Larry Feil

DATE DUE

BRODART, CO.   Cat. No. 23-221-003

playing

social

and

recreational

instruments

playing
social
and
recreational
instruments

ROBERT W. JOHN

CHARLES H. DOUGLAS

University of Georgia
Athens, Georgia

prentice-hall, inc., englewood cliffs, new jersey

Printed in the United States of America

ISBN: 0-13-683680-1

Library of Congress Catalog Card No.: 73-173248

10 9 8 7 6 5 4 3 2 1

PRENTICE-HALL INTERNATIONAL, INC., London
PRENTICE-HALL OF AUSTRALIA, PTY. LTD., Sydney
PRENTICE-HALL OF CANADA, LTD., Toronto
PRENTICE-HALL OF INDIA PRIVATE LIMITED, New Delhi
PRENTICE-HALL OF JAPAN, INC., Tokyo

contents

THE RECORDER 31

THE TONETTE 42

SONGS TO PLAY AND SING 51

APPENDIX 105

introduction

Much of the enjoyment of music is in the action. While there is a place for passive listening and reflection, the music time is normally one of activity and participation. The students sing, they move and dance to music, they play various kinds of musical instruments—from crude, improvised rhythm instruments to the highly sophisticated ones. Great pleasure is derived from *participation* in making music.

Those responsible for the musical education of teachers and social service leaders have found that methods that emphasize the *active* approach help to insure a continuance of musical action and pleasure in their groups. The advent of "social instruments" has made such musical participation easier than ever before. With very little musical understanding and experience one can accompany a song on an Autoharp. The impact on a group of such an active musical role for the leader can be very great.

This book is a manual and guide on how to play several of the more popular social instruments. Its primary purpose is to get "into the action" as quickly and meaningfully as possible. The book, therefore, is for a "user" rather than a "reader." Instruction is presented in simple, succinct, graphic terms. It is expected that an instrument will be used immediately in conjunction with the book.

Instruction is purposely terminated after the basic concepts have been presented. It is a first book—nothing more. Delving into advanced instruction for any of the instruments would negate our intentions. There are advanced instruction books in most of these areas if continued instruction is wanted.

The self satisfying enjoyment one receives in being able to accompany oneself in song on the guitar or the Autoharp is boundless. To share such a pleasure with others is a very special reward for being a teacher or social leader.

The subtle pleasure of "picking out" a melody on the Tonette or recorder is, for those who have never known it, a delight worth working toward. It is the sincere hope of the authors that many such moments of pleasure will result as one moves through the pages of this manual.

R.W.J.
C.H.D.

playing

social

and

recreational

instruments

the

guitar

choosing a guitar

Guitars are available in many different kinds, styles, and makes. Because of its expressiveness and flexibility, the Spanish six-string guitar is recommended as the one most suitable for playing folk music. Since nothing is more discouraging to the beginner than struggling with a cheap, poorly made instrument, it is often better to postpone guitar study until a suitable instrument can be found. When purchasing a guitar, consider these several points:

1. The guitar should have a round hole, nylon strings, and a wide fingerboard (approximately two inches at the nut).
2. The guitar should be tunable. Press down a string at the 12th fret (where the neck joins the body) and pluck the string. Then pluck the same string open. The two sounds should be the same, one an octave higher than the other.
3. The tuning pegs should turn fairly easily, and the metal frets should be smooth and of even height.
4. The top of the guitar should be made of spruce with the lines of the grain evenly spaced. The fingerboard should not be warped. There should be wooden braces underneath the top; these can be felt through the sound hole.
5. All joints of the guitar should be checked for tightness. There should also be no splits in the top, bottom, or sides.
6. A guitar case is a good investment.

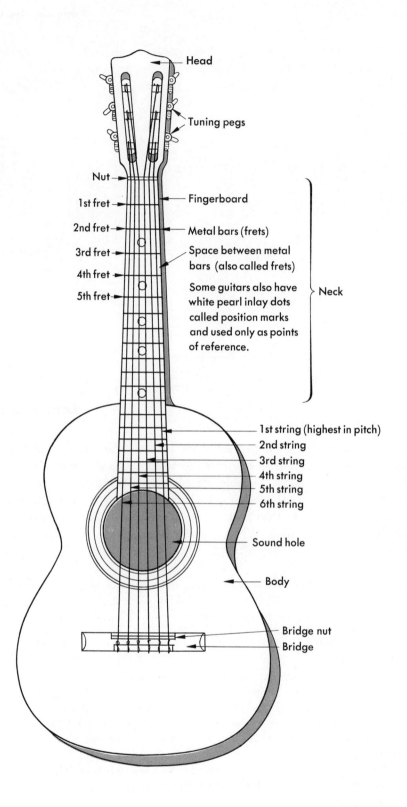

Head

Tuning pegs

Nut

1st fret

2nd fret

3rd fret

4th fret

5th fret

Fingerboard

Metal bars (frets)

Space between metal bars (also called frets)

Some guitars also have white pearl inlay dots called position marks and used only as points of reference.

Neck

1st string (highest in pitch)
2nd string
3rd string
4th string
5th string
6th string

Sound hole

Body

Bridge nut
Bridge

The guitar may be tuned by matching each string with its corresponding note on the piano. The matching is done by tightening or loosening the guitar strings with the tuning pegs until each guitar string sounds like its corresponding piano note.

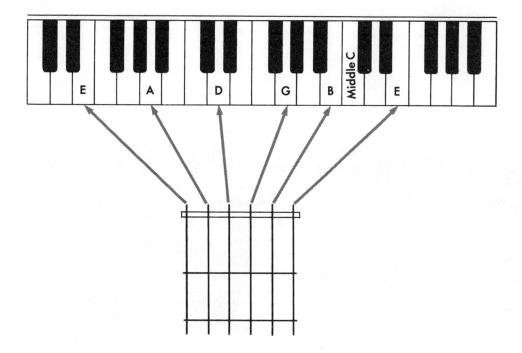

A second method of tuning the guitar is to use a pitch pipe. The pitch pipe for the guitar has six pipes, one for each string of the guitar. Tuning is done by matching each string of the guitar to its corresponding pipe.

To check the tuning of the guitar, stop (i.e., press) the lowest (6th) string just to the left of the 5th fret with the index finger of the left hand, then sound the string with the right hand thumb. Next, sound the open 5th string (i.e., without its being touched by the left hand). The two sounds should be the same. Repeat the procedure for each pair of strings:

The 6th string stopped at the 5th fret should sound the same as the open 5th string.

The 5th string stopped at the 5th fret should sound the same as the open 4th string.

The 4th string stopped at the 5th fret should sound the same as the open 3rd string.

The 3rd string stopped at the *4th* fret should sound the same as the open 2nd string.

The 2nd string stopped at the 5th fret should sound the same as the open 1st string.

The guitar should rest on the left thigh, with the left leg raised above the horizontal position by using a small footstool, books, chair rung, or whatever is handy. The guitar touches the right thigh, adding support. The guitar should be held close to the body in an upright position.

Photographs by Dale Davis, unless otherwise noted.

4

Music is made up of melody, harmony, and rhythm. When folk music is performed, the melody is sung, and the harmony and the rhythm are played on the guitar.

harmony

The harmony is supplied by playing a chord. A chord is usually three or more notes sounded at the same time. Chords have names. To play a simplified C chord, stop (i.e., press) the 2nd string just to the left of the 1st fret with the index finger of the left hand (LH). Using the outside of the right hand (RH) thumb, strum the top three strings with a downward motion of the thumb. If the sound is unpleasant, check to make sure that the LH index finger is touching only the 2nd string.

The simplified C chord just played can be diagramed as follows:

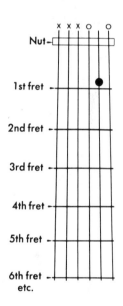

The vertical lines represent the six strings of the guitar.

The horizontal lines represent the frets.

The "x" indicates that the string is not to be sounded.

The "o" indicates that the string is sounded open.

The "•" indicates where the string is stopped by a LH finger.

To play a simplified G⁷ chord, stop the 1st string just to the left of the 1st fret with the index finger of the LH. Again strum the top three strings with the right thumb. The simplified G⁷ chord can be diagramed as follows:

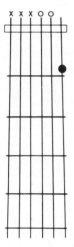

Play the C chord, then the G⁷ chord, then back to the C chord. Do this until you can move from one to the other with ease.

rhythm

The rhythm of a song is the beat used to accompany the melody. In the following song, the beats are indicated by arrows above the words. While singing the song, clap your hands together for each arrow.

$$\downarrow \qquad \downarrow \qquad \downarrow \qquad \downarrow$$
Flies in the buttermilk, shoo fly shoo,
$$\downarrow \qquad \downarrow \qquad \downarrow \qquad \downarrow$$
Flies in the buttermilk, shoo fly shoo,
$$\downarrow \qquad \downarrow \qquad \downarrow \qquad \downarrow$$
Flies in the buttermilk, shoo fly shoo,
$$\downarrow \qquad \downarrow \qquad \downarrow \downarrow$$
Skip to my Lou, my darling.

playing a song

Sing "Skip to My Lou" again and this time substitute the guitar strum for the clapping of hands. The chord name has been substituted for the arrow. Be sure that the LH index finger changes at the right time so as to produce the given chord.

```
        C              C            C           C
Flies in the buttermilk, shoo fly shoo,
        G⁷             G⁷           G⁷          G⁷
Flies in the buttermilk, shoo fly shoo,
        C              C            C           C
Flies in the buttermilk, shoo fly shoo,
        G⁷             G⁷        C C
Skip to my Lou, my darling.
```

The accompaniment in music notation looks like this (**/** = thumb strum):

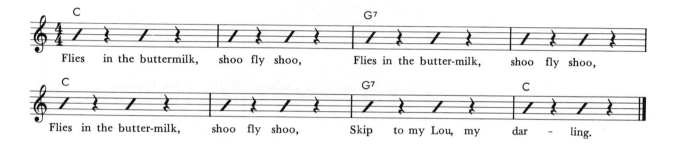

other songs

Many songs can be played using only the two chords just learned. Some suggestions:

"Billy Boy," page 57
"Bold Soldier," page 60
"Deaf Woman's Courtship," page 66
"Green Corn," page 74
"Gypsy Davey," page 76
"Putting on the Style," page 92

a more interesting accompaniment

A more interesting accompaniment can be accomplished by playing a low note, called a bass note, followed by a chord. The bass note for a C chord is produced by placing the ring finger of the LH on the 5th string, 3rd fret, and playing the note with the RH thumb. The diagram of the C chord now looks like this:

7

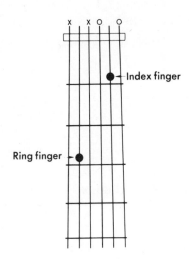

To play the chord following the bass note, place the RH index finger on the 3rd string, the RH middle finger on the 2nd string, and the RH ring finger on the 1st string. Play the chord by closing the RH toward the position of a fist, plucking all three strings at the same time.

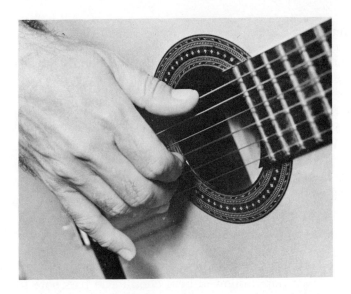

Form a C chord with the LH. Play the bass note (5th string) with the RH thumb, then play the top three strings simultaneously with the RH index, middle, and ring fingers. Then play the bass note again followed by the plucked chord. Practice this bass-chord alternation until it becomes smooth and even.

In music notation:

The bass note for a G⁷ chord is produced by placing the LH ring finger on the 6th string, 3rd fret. The diagram of the G⁷ chord now looks like this:

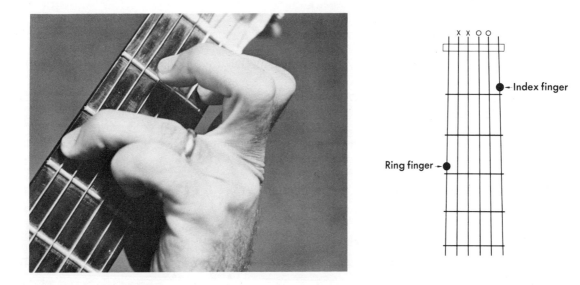

Form a G⁷ chord with the LH. Play the bass note (6th string) with the RH thumb, then pluck the top three strings. Practice this bass-chord alternation until it can be done with ease.

In music notation:

Play the song "Skip to My Lou" using the bass-chord alternation (b = bass, c = chord).

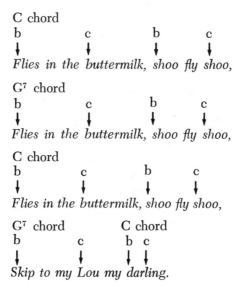

```
C chord
b          c          b          c
↓          ↓          ↓          ↓
Flies in the buttermilk, shoo fly shoo,

G⁷ chord
b          c          b          c
↓          ↓          ↓          ↓
Flies in the buttermilk, shoo fly shoo,

C chord
b          c          b          c
↓          ↓          ↓          ↓
Flies in the buttermilk, shoo fly shoo,

G⁷ chord          C chord
b          c      b  c
↓          ↓      ↓  ↓
Skip to my Lou my darling.
```

In music notation:

Flies in the buttermilk, shoo fly shoo,   Flies in the buttermilk, shoo fly shoo,

Flies in the buttermilk,   shoo fly shoo,   Skip to my Lou   my   dar - ling.

Now play the same song with the same type of accompaniment, but with the rhythm moving twice as fast.

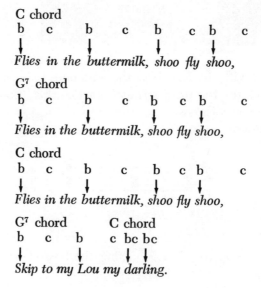

C chord
b   c   b   c   b   c   b   c
Flies in the buttermilk, shoo fly shoo,

G⁷ chord
b   c   b   c   b   c   b   c
Flies in the buttermilk, shoo fly shoo,

C chord
b   c   b   c   b   c   b   c
Flies in the buttermilk, shoo fly shoo,

G⁷ chord   C chord
b   c   b   c bc bc
Skip to my Lou my darling.

In music notation:

Flies in the butter-milk,   shoo fly shoo,   Flies in the butter milk,   shoo fly shoo,

Flies in the butter-milk,   shoo fly shoo,   Skip to my Lou   my   dar — ling.

Play the other suggested songs that use only two chords.

Up to this point, you have been playing in duple meter. To play in triple meter, play the bass note followed by two plucked chords instead of one.
In music notation:

Song Suggestions

"Clementine," page **64**
"Down in the Valley," page **67**
"Oh, Dear, What Can the Matter Be?" page **88**

playing in the key of G

You have been playing in the key of "C." Because of their range, some songs are easier to sing in one key than they are in another. To play "Skip to My Lou" in the key of "G," two new chords must be learned, the G chord and the D⁷ chord. The G chord is not the same as the G⁷ chord you have already learned. Look at the diagram for the G chord.

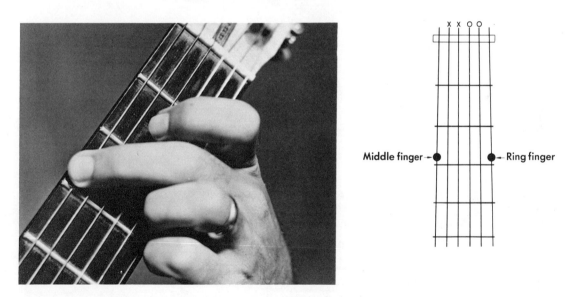

As you did for the C and G⁷ chords, play the bass note (6th string) followed by the chord.
In music notation:

The diagram for the D⁷ chord looks like this:

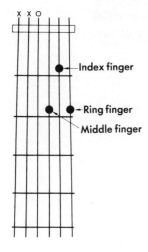

The bass note for the D⁷ chord is the open 4th string. Play this chord, alternating the bass note with the chord.

In music notation:

Play "Skip to My Lou" once more, this time in the key of G.

> G
> *Flies in the buttermilk, shoo fly shoo,*
> D⁷
> *Flies in the buttermilk, shoo fly shoo,*
> G
> *Flies in the buttermilk, shoo fly shoo,*
> D⁷   G
> *Skip to my Lou, my darling.*

Many songs can be played with the four chords you have already learned.

Song Suggestions

playing alternate bass notes

Alternate bass notes may be used to add interest to your song accompaniments. You have already learned a bass note for each chord that you play. Each of these chords also has an alternate bass note.

Chord Name	Bass Note	Alternate Bass Note
C	5th string, 3rd fret Played with ring finger	6th string, 3rd fret Played with ring finger
G7	6th string, 3rd fret Played with ring finger	4th string, open
G	6th string, 3rd fret Played with middle finger	4th string, open
D7	4th string, open	5th string, open

To use the alternate bass in duple time, play the bass note, then the chord, then the alternate bass note, then the chord again.

In music notation:

To use the alternate bass in triple time, play the bass note followed by the chord played twice, then the alternate bass note followed by the chord played twice.

In music notation:

playing in a minor key

Some songs are written in minor keys. One of these minor keys is the key of A minor. Play the A minor chord given in the following diagram.

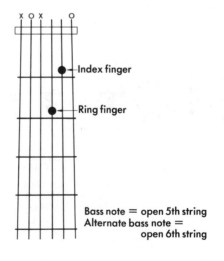

Index finger

Ring finger

Bass note = open 5th string
Alternate bass note =
                open 6th string

14

A chord usually found in the key of A minor is the E chord.

Song Suggestions

"Drill, Ye Tarriers, Drill," 68
"Greensleeves," 76
"Hunchback Fiddler," 78

returning to the key of C

By learning the F chord and using the chords already learned, you can play several new songs. Note the F chord diagram; the LH index finger stops both the 1st and 2nd strings on the 1st fret.

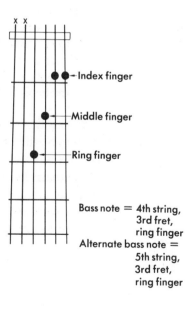

playing the arpeggio strum

The arpeggio strum is performed by playing only one note at a time with the right hand. To play in triple meter, first play the bass note with the thumb, then the 3rd string with the index finger, next the 2nd string with the middle finger, then the 1st string with the ring finger, next the 2nd string with the middle finger, and then the 3rd string with the index finger. Six separate sounds should be heard in each measure.

In music notation:

To play the arpeggio strum in duple meter, first play the bass note with the thumb, then the 3rd string with the index finger, next the 2nd string with the middle finger, then the 1st string with the ring finger, next play the alternate bass note with the thumb, then the 3rd string, then the 2nd string, and finally the 1st string. Eight separate sounds should be heard in each measure.

In music notation:

Song Suggestions

playing bass runs

To add variety to your accompaniments, bass runs may be used. A bass run is a series of single notes used to move from one chord to another. These notes are substituted for the last few beats of a measure; they are played with the RH thumb.

If a C chord is given for four beats, followed by an F chord, play the bass note of the C chord (using the RH thumb) on the first beat, then the top three strings together on the second beat (index, middle, and ring fingers). On the third beat play the open 4th string with the RH thumb, then stop the 4th string, 2nd fret, with the LH middle finger and play this note with the RH thumb on the fourth beat. The F chord is then played as usual—bass note, chord, etc.

In music notation:

If an F chord is given for four beats, followed by a G⁷ chord, play the bass note of the F chord on the first beat, then pluck the top three strings together on the second beat. On the third beat play the 6th string, 1st fret, index finger with the RH thumb, then on the fourth beat play the 6th string, 2nd fret, middle finger with the RH thumb. The G⁷ chord is then played as usual.

In music notation:

If a G⁷ chord is given for four beats, followed by a C chord, play the bass note of the G⁷ chord on the first beat, then pluck the top three strings together on the second beat. On the third beat play the open 5th string with the RH thumb. On the fourth beat play the 5th string, 2nd fret, middle finger with the RH thumb. The C chord is then played as usual.

In music notation:

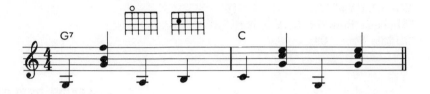

The song used to illustrate the use of bass runs is "Foggy, Foggy Dew" (page 72). The beats are shown by the chord names and arrows. On each given chord name play the bass note of the given chord.

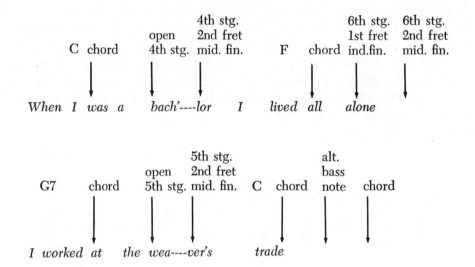

In music notation:

"Abdullah Bulbul Amir," 53
"Bile Them Cabbage Down," 56
"Can't You Dance the Polka?" 62
"Cindy," 63
"Eliza Jane," 69
"Oh, Mary, Don't You Weep," 89
"Paper of Pins," 91
"Putting on the Style," 92
"So Long, It's Been Good to Know You," 96

For those students interested in playing more songs, the following list of books is suggested.

American Folk Songs. Baltimore: Penguin Books, Inc., 1964.

Dallin, Leon and Lynn, eds., *Folk Songster.* Dubuque, Iowa: Wm. C. Brown Company, 1967.

Folk Song Jamboree. New York: Ballantine Books, Inc., 1960.

Guitarfest. Bryn Mawr, Pa.: Theodore Presser Company, 1967.

Ives, Burl, *Burl Ives Song Book.* New York: Ballantine Books, Inc., 1953.

————, *More Burl Ives Songs.* New York: Ballantine Books, Inc., 1966.

Leisy, J., ed., *Songs for Pickin' and Singin'.* New York: Fawcett World Library, 1962.

Sharp, C., and M. Karpeles, eds., *Eighty English Folk Songs from the Southern Appalachians.* Cambridge, Mass.: MIT Press, 1969.

Song Fest. New York: Crown Publishers, Inc., 1955.

For those students interested in more advanced guitar techniques, the following list of books is suggested.

Filiberto, R., *Folk Guitar Styles.* Kirkwood, Missouri: Mel Bay Publications.

Lee, R., *Folk Strums for Guitar.* New York: Sam Fox Publishing.

————, and H. David, *More Strums for Guitar.* New York: Sam Fox Publishing.

Noad, F., *The Guitar Songbook.* New York: Crowell Collier and Macmillan, Inc., 1969.

————, *Playing the Guitar.* New York: Crowell Collier and Macmillan, Inc., 1965

Silverman, J., *The Art of the Folk-Blues Guitar.* New York: Oak Publications, Inc., 1964.

————, *Beginning the Folk Guitar.* New York: Oak Publications, Inc.

————, *The Folksinger's Guitar Guide.* New York: Oak Publications, Inc.

the

Autoharp*

The Autoharp is a stringed instrument widely used in the classroom. The combination of portability and ease of playing make it an ideal instrument for the teacher to use in accompanying singing. Its pleasant, quiet tone adds much to the enrichment of a song. Because of its unique construction, the Autoharp can be played effectively with only minimum instruction and practice.

There are many different types and models of the instrument, ranging from the most simple twelve-chord bar types to those which contain a great number of such chord bars. In recent times it has been popular to amplify the tone of the instrument by means of attached electronic equipment. The instrument these authors found to be most satisfactory for general-purpose classroom use is the fifteen-bar (non-amplified) Autoharp.

It is strongly recommended that a case be purchased with the instrument. The few dollars extra one pays for the case is a very worthwhile investment. A sturdy case will guard the instrument from possible transport damage and also serve as a convenient carrying vehicle.

the picks

It is quite possible to strum the Autoharp with fingers only, and in some advanced forms of strumming it is preferred. It is more common, however, for standard playing, to use a *pick*.

---

* Although the term *Autoharp* is commonly used to describe all instruments of this type, regardless of manufacturer, the name is actually a registered trademark name of Oscar Schmidt, International, Inc., of Union, New Jersey.

The two most common types of picks are (1) those made of a stiff felt, which produce a soft muted effect when used, and (2) those made of plastic or celluloid, which produce a crisp, sharp, loud sound. Which pick to use will depend on the type of music and the occasion for which the instrument will be used.

the tuning key

The instrument is furnished with a tuning key, which looks something like a modified roller-skate key. Tuning the instrument is discussed later in this chapter.

playing the instrument

The easiest and most widely used position for playing the Autoharp is to place the instrument in front of you on a desk or table top with the long, straight side of the instrument closest to you. Adjust the instrument to a slight angle so that the chord bars can be fingered comfortably.

Autoharp on table in front of player

Now, place your *left hand* on the chord bar projections. Use your first three fingers. Hold the pick with your right hand, between the thumb and first finger, and reach across the left hand (cross-over) and strum the strings upward—that is, away from the body—to the left of the set of chord bars. This cross-over method of strumming is the most popular.

It is possible (and sometimes done) to strum the strings to the right of the chord bar, thus avoiding crossing hands. Most people feel that a better tone can be produced when the center of the strings is strummed than can be produced if the string is strummed very near its end. For this reason, although it feels a bit awkward at first, most players prefer the cross-over method.

Holding the pick and cross-over strum

the carry

Although this method of playing the Autoharp is usually considered only after the player has had considerable experience in playing the instrument as it lies flat in front of him, there is no reason why the novice cannot, if he wishes, begin with the carry method. As shown in the photo, this method of holding the instrument calls for the player to cradle it in the left arm and finger the chord bars with the left hand, and strum the strings with the right hand. The obvious advantage to the teacher in playing the instrument in this manner is that she can move about while playing. Most people find it best to postpone this method of playing until experience has been gained playing it in the flat position.

The carry position

accompanying a song

We will begin by accompanying a song written in F Major. Other keys can be used, but the chord bars most used when playing in F Major are near the center of the instrument—easy to play and easy to read.

1. Push down the chord bar marked *F Maj.* Do this with the index finger of the left hand.
2. At the same time, lightly touch, but *do not push down,* the chord bars marked C[7] and B♭ Maj. In the key of F these are the primary chords.
3. Now, with your right hand, holding the felt pick, reach across your left hand, and give an upward sweep of *all* the strings. Upward in this case means away from the body. If the *F Maj.* chord bar is properly depressed, only the strings of the F Major chord (F, A, and C) will sound. The felt attached to the underside of the chord bar will suppress or dampen all other strings.
4. Establish a slow, even "beat" by repeating a series of sweeps on F Major. As you do this sing the following songs.

ARE YOU SLEEPING?

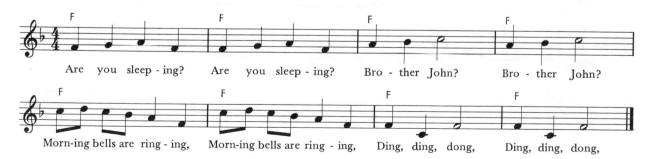

GRANDMA JONES

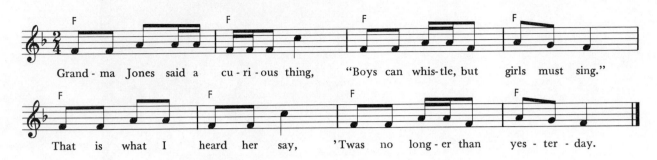

Grand - ma Jones said a cu - ri - ous thing, "Boys can whis-tle, but girls must sing."

That is what I heard her say, 'Twas no long-er than yes - ter-day.

THE LONE STAR TRAIL

I start - ed up the trail on June twen-ty - third, I been

punch - in' Tex - as cat - tle on the Lone Star Trail, Sing - in'

Ki - yi yip - pi yap - pi yay, yap - pi yay! Sing - in'

Ki - yi yip - yi yap - pi yay!—————

Now try the key of C Major.

ROW, ROW, ROW YOUR BOAT

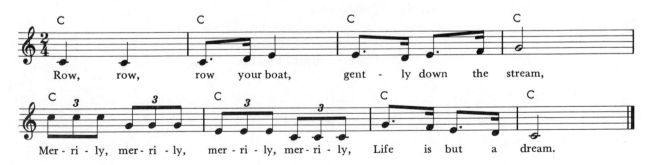

Row, row, row your boat, gent - ly down the stream,

Mer - ri - ly, mer - ri - ly, mer - ri - ly, mer - ri - ly, Life is but a dream.

24

In these four songs, only a single chord was used throughout each song. If all songs used only one chord, music would sound frightfully monotonous. Most songs, therefore, need more than a single chord to serve as an accompaniment. Many songs—a surprising number—use only three chords. These chords, built on the first, fourth, and fifth degrees of the scale, are known as the *primary* chords. Before we sing and play songs using all three primary chords, let us try some which contain only two chords. The song "Tom Dooley" is easy to play because the first half of the song can be sung with an F Major chord accompaniment, and the latter half with C^7 chord. It should be noted that most songs of the type contained in this book and in most children's songbooks start and stop on the "key" chord—known as the *tonic* chord. It is necessary, therefore, at the very end of the song "Tom Dooley" to return (or cadence) to the tonic chord (F Major).

TOM DOOLEY

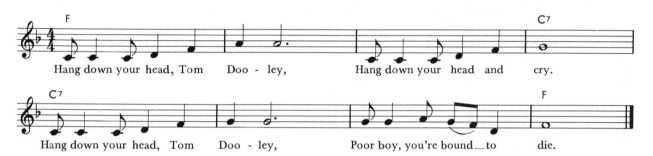

Also try this two-chord song. Keep a beat with your right-hand sweeps and hold down the same chord bar until there is an indication to change. Use your index finger for the F Major bar and have ready (lightly touching but not pressing) your middle finger on the C^7 bar. Change chords where indicated.

AUNT RHODY

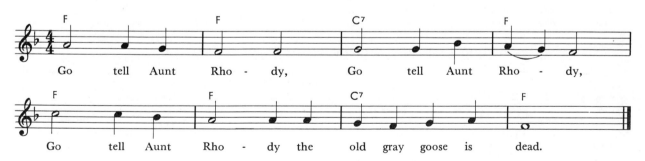

If the song you wish to sing doesn't "feel right" because it is pitched either too high or too low, change it! This is known as *transposition*. Notice in the song "Aunt Rhody" the key or tonic chord was F Major. The other chord was a C⁷ chord, which is built on the fifth degree of the F scale. The chord on the fifth degree is called the *dominant* chord. Let us raise the pitch of this song one step by making G Major (instead of F Major) the key chord. If G is tonic, then the dominant of G (fifth) is D or D⁷. Try "Aunt Rhody" in the key of G. Use G and D⁷ instead of F and C⁷.

Should you want the song pitched lower, just lower the tonic chord to whatever pitch seems suitable, and find your relative dominant chord. Remember, the dominant chord is the fifth of the scale. If, for example, you decide to make C your key chord, then the fifth of C is G. (Most dominant chords are seventh chords, so on the Autoharp, the dominant of C is G⁷.)

Strum a series of tonic and dominant chords in the key in which you plan to sing the song. This will give you a tonal feeling for the key. Once this is established, sing the song in the new key.

Here are other songs which contain but two chords—tonic and dominant. Try them in the key in which they are written and in any other (major) key which seems suitable to your voice. Remember, the dominant is the fifth degree of the key.

SAVEZ–VOUS?

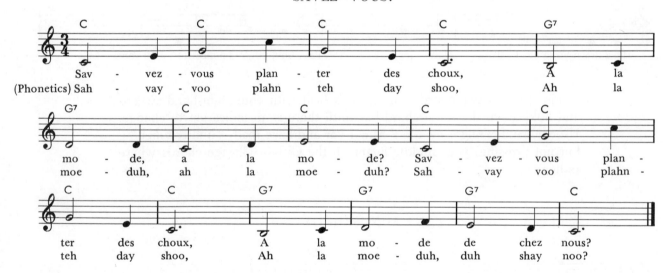

HE'S GOT THE WHOLE WORLD IN HIS HANDS

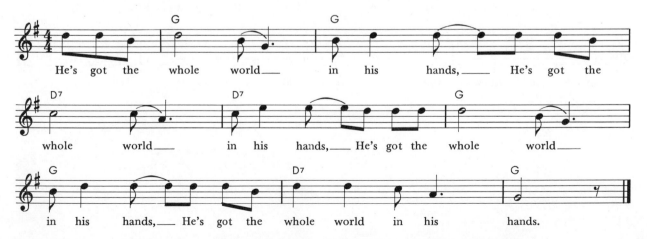

Only one three-chord song is given here because many more can be found later in the book. The third chord of the primary group of chords (in addition to the tonic and dominant) is the *subdominant*, built on the fourth degree of the scale. Learn this chart, and apply it to the Autoharp.

Key (or Tonic) Chord	Subdominant Chord	Dominant Chord
F Major	B♭ Major	C7
C Major	F Major	G7
G Major	C Major	D7
B♭ Major *	E♭ Major	F7
A Minor	D Minor	E7
D Minor	G Minor	A7
D Major *	G Major	A7

BINGO

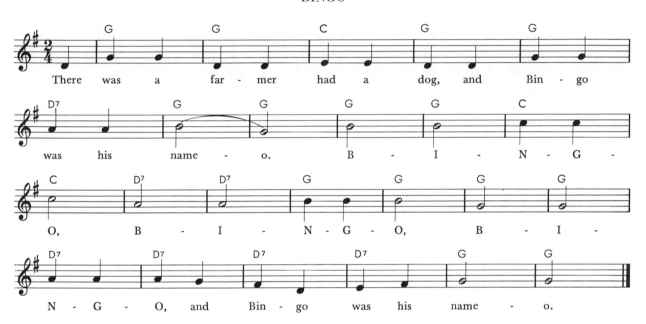

strumming techniques and variations

Little has been said to now about specific strumming techniques. Beginning students, be they children or adults, should be allowed considerable freedom in this matter. The Autoharp is capable of serving two major purposes—one is to give chordal support to a melody, and the other to impart a feeling of rhythm. Any method of playing the instrument which can accomplish these ends is justifiable. Listed below are a few ways this can be done. The list is basic and rudimentary. The student should experiment with all of these methods, plus those he improvises. He will soon discover that in most cases the mood of the song will dictate the type of strumming which sounds best for that particular song.

---

* These chord series are not possible on the twelve-bar Autoharp. The D Major primary chords (D Major, A[7], and G Major) are playable on all instruments larger than the twelve-bar ones, but because of the distance between chord bars, it is suggested that here the middle finger play the D bar, the index finger the A[7] bar, and the thumb play the G Major bar.

strumming method number one

This is a full upward sweep of all of the strings of the instrument on each beat of the measure. This soon gets to be a bit overpowering and tiring for both the player and the listener.

    / / /   / / /   / /
Are you sleep - ing, Are you sleep - ing,

    /   / /   / / /
Broth - er John? Broth - er John?

method number two

This method is similar to the first, in that it calls for a full sweep of all of the strings, but instead of sweeping on every beat, now the strum comes only on the first beat of the measure. This presumes that the harmony will remain constant through the full measure. When this is not true—more likely in 4/4 and 6/8 songs—then the strum should be also on the secondary beat or whatever beats demand a change in harmony. Strumming on the first beat of the measure is especially effective in many 2/4 and 3/4 songs.

    /   /
Are you sleep - ing, Are you sleep - ing,

    /   /
Broth - er John? Broth - er John?

or

    /   /
Lost my part - ner, What'll I do?

    /   /
Lost my part - ner, What'll I do?

    /   /
Lost my part - ner, What'll I do?

    /   /
Skip to my Lou, my dar - ling.

method number three

With this method, only the very low strings are strummed on the first beat of the measure, and the higher strings are strummed on other beats. This can give a marked, "um-pah" rhythmical effect.

    /   /   /   /
Lost my part - ner, What'll I do?

    /   /   /   /
Lost my part - ner, What'll I do?

    /   /   /   /
Lost my part - ner, What'll I do?

    /   /   /   /
Skip to my Lou, my dar - ling.

method number four

Here the full set of strings is divided into roughly three sections—the low section, the middle section, and the high section. Now the low strings are strummed on the first beat of the measure, and the other two sections of the instrument are strummed on the other beats. On certain songs, this can be most effective.

melody strumming

A more advanced technique of playing the Autoharp is known as *melody strumming*. This method differs from chord strumming in several ways. If a pick is used, which is optional, it is usually a thumb pick. Very often no pick is used, but the strumming is done either with the thumb or with the index finger. The technique is to terminate the strum on the melody note. This is done by giving careful attention to the names and numbers of each string—as printed on the instrument. This manner of playing the Autoharp is beyond the limits of this book.*

tuning the Autoharp

The Autoharp is tuned by means of a tuning key, furnished with the instrument. The key fits the square pegs or pins which support the strings. Most of the time, the string, if it is out of tune, will sound too low. If this is the case, it must be tightened, thus pulling it up to pitch. Pluck the string and tighten the string slightly. Do this by turning the key in a clockwise direction. Use an accurate pitch as your model—such as the same tone on a (well tuned) piano or pitch pipe.

* A good advanced book on the Autoharp is *Autoharp, Advanced Technique*, Vol. 2, by Meg Peterson, published by Oscar Schmidt International, Inc., 1966.

There are several correct methods for tuning the entire instrument. Each player soon decides which method he prefers. Any method which gets the Autoharp in tune is an acceptable method.

The tuning method we have found to be the easiest and fastest is to tune all tones of the same letter name in order. That is, start on C and tune all C's (octaves). Then go to G, and tune all G's. Once these are tuned, go to all E's. When this is done, you will have the C chord in tune. Now use G as your reference point and tune a fifth above G—or D. Next B. This will give you another complete chord (G Major). Now the only natural tones remaining to be tuned are F and A. Play C again, and think of the NBC chimes. This will assist in tuning the F's and A's. (The "chimes" N-B-C sound the intervals of C-A-F.)

Some players prefer to make a straight comparison with pitches taken from the piano or pitch pipe. Play a note on a (tuned) piano, play the same note on the Autoharp, and compare pitches. Frequently, it will not be necessary to retune the entire instrument, but merely "touch up" those strings which are not in proper tune. A slow, deliberate strum with any chord bar depressed will help in deciding which tones are out of tune.

Much of the fun of playing the instrument is lost if it is not in proper tune. If you find it doesn't sound right, ask for help. A music teacher or a player of a guitar or most any other stringed instrument can probably tune the instrument. If none of these people is available, take the instrument to a local piano store and for a nominal fee, the piano tuner will tune and adjust it for you. The pleasure of playing a well tuned and regulated instrument will more than compensate for the small expense of having the instrument put in fine playing condition.

the

recorder

There are many sizes and types of recorders, but those most widely used are:

1. *The Soprano Recorder*, pitched in C. This is the most popular of the recorders, and the one for which this chapter is written.
2. *The Alto Recorder*, pitched in F. This instrument is a bit larger than the Soprano, and as its name implies, can produce tones a bit lower than the smaller Soprano. Recently very satisfactory plastic Alto Recorders have been produced and it is quite possible that this instrument may become increasingly popular.
3. *The Tenor Recorder*, pitched in C. This instrument is larger than either the Soprano or the Alto Recorder. In fact, it is most common to have key extensions on the Tenor Recorder. This means that some of the tone holes are covered by means of a key mechanism rather than by the direct contact of the finger. Fingerings for the Tenor Recorder are the same as those for the Soprano Recorder.
4. *The Bass Recorder*, pitched in F. The lowest pitched instrument of the family, the Bass Recorder is usually played with the assistance of a bocal, or some type of mouthpipe extension. Without it, it would be impossible for the average person to manipulate this instrument if held similar to the other three sizes of instruments.

The soprano and tenor recorders can play all of the music in this book which is within range of the instruments. The alto and bass recorders must transpose, however. A fingering chart is available for both groups of recorders.

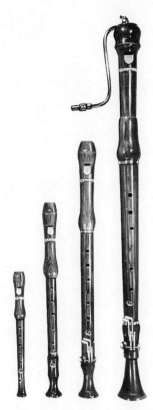

Courtesy of Trophy Music Co., Cleveland, Ohio.

advantages in playing the recorder

1. Unlike most other wind instruments, no embouchure problems are involved in playing the recorder. The fipple mouthpiece requires no specially developed skill to play.
2. The tone is soft and sonorous.
3. The range is considerably extended over the limited range of the whistle flutes.
4. There is a large body of music already written for the recorder. The performance of recorder music both in solo form and in ensembles is a practice of long standing.
5. The instruments are simply constructed, therefore are inexpensive. Recent improvements of plastic recorders make them an excellent choice for school use. Plastic instruments require very little maintenance, and by simple sterilization of the instruments, can be used by succession of classes.
6. Because of their simplicity, success on the instrument can be achieved with far less practice and effort than on most band or orchestra instruments.

when to begin

Most music educators feel that at about the fourth or fifth grade the child is ready to begin playing the recorder. The most critical physical need is that the child can reach and cover the tone holes.

The soprano recorder may come in one, two, or three parts, depending on the maker and the material. If the instrument has more than one part, the parts should be put together with a gentle twisting motion. The finger holes should line up with the "window" of the head joint. If there is a third part —a foot joint—it should be a bit off to the right to allow the little finger to more easily cover the holes.

holding the instrument

The instrument is held so that the fingers of the left hand will be used to cover the tone holes of the *upper* portion of the instrument, and the fingers of the right hand will cover the *lower* portion.

The thumb of the left hand covers the hole on the back of the instrument. This tone hole remains covered for most of the tones, although it will be off for some and will be half covered for others. Notice that the index finger covers tone hole 1, the middle finger covers tone hole 2, and the ring finger covers tone hole 3. The little finger of the left hand is not used in playing the recorder.

playing the instrument

With your left hand, cover the following tone holes: Thumb (T), 1, 2, and 3. Place the mouthpiece of the instrument on the lower lip, and gently bite down on the top of the instrument. Be sure to allow free passage of air through the air duct at the end of the instrument. Start a tone in a manner similar to the way you might say the word "too." Do not merely push the breath through the instrument, but use your tongue as a valve to start and stop the air flow. A "too" will produce a sharp, crisp beginning or attack of a tone. A "doo" will produce a softer attack. Blow easily.

the tone G

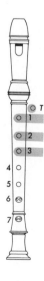

Play this tone several times to determine the amount of air necessary to produce a clear tone. The instrument is inherently a quiet instrument, so do not overblow in an attempt to get more volume of sound.

Make certain that all tone holes are tightly covered. Use the fleshy "ball" of the finger—not the tip—to cover each tone hole. Keep the fingers close to the tone holes when they are not in use. This will reduce the finger movement distance when the holes must be covered.

Repeat the tone G. This time, start the tone with the help of the tongue. Say (or think) "too" each time you begin a tone.

Too   Too   Too   Too

the tone A

To play the tone A, repeat the tone G and then lift the ring finger. The tone A is produced by covering tone holes T, 1, and 2.

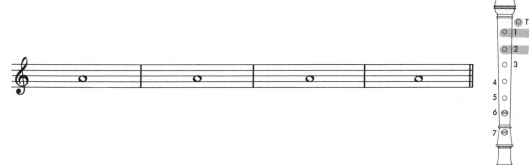

the tone B

Play the tone A again as above, and to play B merely lift the middle finger. The tone B is produced by covering tone holes T and 1.

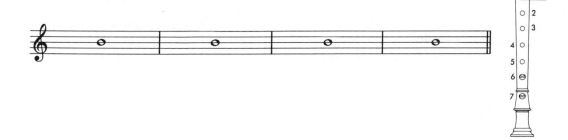

exercises using the tones G, A, and B

Play as many of these exercises as you feel necessary to insure complete familiarity with the tones G, A, and B.

add the right hand

While there is much good logic in continuing to remove fingers of the left hand and teach the tones high C and D at this time, it is probably better to postpone these tones until later. Removing all fingers makes it very difficult to control the holding of the instrument, especially for children.

the tone (low) C

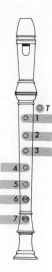

This is the lowest tone playable on the recorder. It is produced by covering all of the tone holes, namely T, 1, 2, 3, 4, 5, 6, and 7. Because so many tone holes need covering there is a greater possibility that some hole will not be correctly covered, thus producing either no tone at all or a faulty tone. Remember, any slight opening of a tone hole will result in faulty tones. Also, blow easily. It is a common fault to overblow the recorder.

the tone F

Although this is not the next tone up, it is probably best introduced at this point because of the fingering. On most recorders, the tone F sounds best when played with the preferred fingering shown. An alternate fingering (which is more logical and a bit easier to execute) unfortunately does not produce a tone F in as clear and in-tune manner as does the first fingering.

Fingering the tone F (preferred method, sometimes called the "Baroque" fingering). Finger the low *C* as above. Now remove only the middle finger of the right hand. The preferred fingering for the tone F is T, 1, 2, 3, 4, 6, and 7.

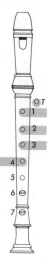

Alternate fingering for the tone F (sometimes called the "German" fingering). With this fingering the tone F is produced by covering tone holes T, 1, 2, 3, and 4.

the tone E

This tone is produced by covering tone holes T, 1, 2, 3, 4, and 5.

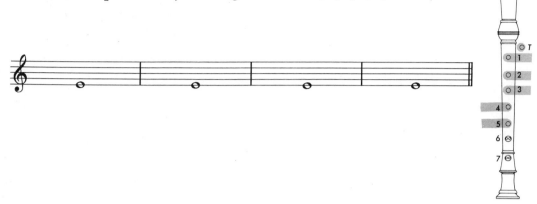

the tone D

Finger and play the tone E above. Now add the ring finger of the right hand. The tone *D* is produced by covering the following tone holes: T, 1, 2, 3, 4, 5, and 6.

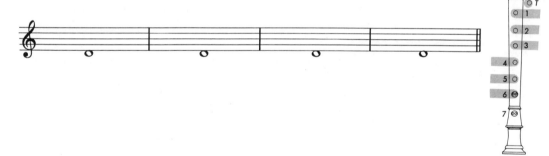

Play the following tunes. Refer back to a fingering only when necessary. Memorize fingerings quickly.

WAYFARING STRANGER

OH, WHEN THE SAINTS

PURPLE SKY

the tone C (third space)

When the student has reached this point of advancement, the tones C and D should be introduced. To control the holding of the instrument when all of the fingers are removed, the sides of the first fingers of each hand, together with the support the lips give the mouthpiece, will keep the instrument in playing position.

The tone C is produced by covering tone holes T and 2. Notice that tone hole 1 is *open*.

the tone D

To play this tone, once again play C as above and now remove the left thumb. The tone D is produced by covering only tone hole 2.

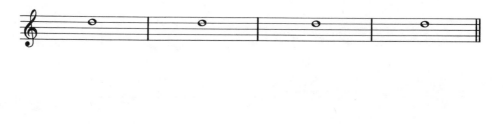

The recorder is capable of playing all of the chromatically altered tones within the extremes of its range. Only the three most commonly used ones are shown here, but one should refer to the fingering chart in the Appendix for all other tones.

the tone B flat

The tone B flat will sound lower than regular B but higher than A. Play the tone B. This is done by covering tone holes T and 1. Now leave tone hole 2 open, but cover the holes 3 and 4. The tone B flat is produced by covering tone holes T, 1, 3, and 4.*

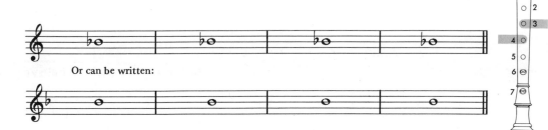

Or can be written:

the tone F sharp

The tone F sharp will sound higher than F but lower than G. To produce this tone, play the tone G (T, 1, 2, and 3), now leave tone hole 4 open, but cover holes 5 and 6. F sharp is produced by covering tone holes T, 1, 2, 3, 5, and 6.*

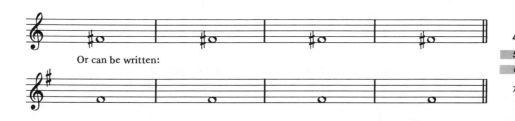

Or can be written:

---

* Another possible fingering is given for this tone in the fingering chart in the Appendix. In cases where alternate fingerings are possible, the one given preference is the easiest to execute, although on some instruments it may not be as exact in pitch. The student should try all possible fingerings and use the one which best suits his purposes.

the tone C sharp

The tone C sharp will sound higher than regular C but lower than D. Finger regular C (T and 2). Now remove 2. C sharp is played by covering only the thumb hole.

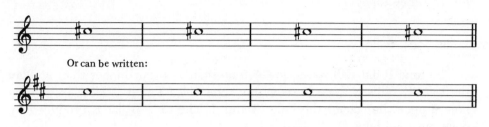

Or can be written:

notes of the second octave

One of the major advantages of the recorder over the plastic whistle flutes is its ability to produce tones in a second register—or octave.

Like the regular transverse flute, the recorder overblows at the octave. This means that, in general, the tones of the second octave are produced by using similar fingering to those of the first octave. The fact is, however, that there are some minor differences. Consult the fingering charts (page 112) for these differences.

To assist the player to produce the "overblown" second octave, the thumb tone hole is only half covered. On some instruments a bit more air is needed to produce tones in the upper octave.

practice second octave tone

Play a tone in the lower octave and, while playing, slide the thumb partly off its tone hole. This should produce the tone in the upper register.

JOHNNY HAS GONE FOR A SOLDIER

GO TELL IT ON THE MOUNTAIN

JACOB'S LADDER

the
Tonette*

holding the instrument

The instrument is held so that the fingers of the left hand will be used to cover the tone holes of the *upper* portion of the instrument, and the fingers of the right hand will cover the *lower* portion.

---

* Commonly used as a generic term to identify all plastic whistle flutes such as the Song-flutes, Flutophone, etc., Tonette is a trade name of an instrument manufactured by the Chicago Musical Instrument Company.

42

The thumb of the left hand covers the hole on the back of the instrument. This tone hole remains covered for most of the tones produced on the instrument. Notice, the index finger covers tone hole 1, the middle finger tone hole 2, and the ring finger covers tone hole 3. The little finger of the left hand is not used in playing these instruments.

Most instruments, regardless of make, have some type of a thumb rest to the rear and slightly below the middle of the instrument. Place the right thumb on this rest. Many people find it more comfortable to use the side of the thumb near the first joint for this support, rather than using the "ball" of the thumb.

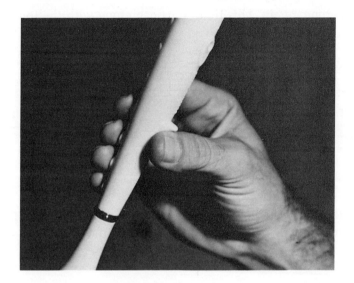

playing the instrument

Cover tone holes T, 1, 2, 3. This produces the tone G. Press your lips around the mouthpiece and gently blow through the instrument. It is not necessary to blow hard; in fact, hard blowing will likely produce a harsh, shrill tone.

the tone G

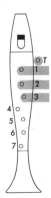

Play several G tones to get the "feel" of producing a tone on the instrument.

Two things are important to notice:

1. If the tone is not clear, either you are blowing too hard into the instrument, or (more likely) you are not covering the tone holes correctly. DO *NOT* USE THE TIPS OF YOUR FINGERS TO COVER THE TONE HOLES. The fleshy "ball" of the finger should be used to close the tone holes in a cushion manner. Even the slightest air leak from a tone hole will result in a bad "squeaky" tone.

2. Instead of merely starting the tone by pushing the breath through the instrument, use the tongue as a "on-off" valve for the air column. Take a big breath, then allow the tongue to control the release of the breath into the instrument. Do this much like you would say "too."

Play the G tones again. This time, start each tone with the tongue. Think "too."

Too   Too   Too   Too

the tone A

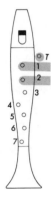

To play the tone A, repeat the tone G and then lift the ring finger. The tone A is produced by covering tone holes T, 1, and 2.

the tone B

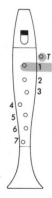

Repeat the tone A and to produce the tone B merely lift the middle finger. The tone B is produced by covering tone holes T and 1.

exercises using the tones G, A, and B

Play as many of the following exercises as you feel necessary to insure complete familiarity with the tones G, A, and B.

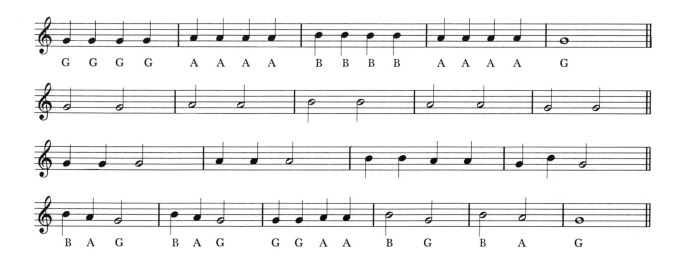

G G G G   A A A A   B B B B   A A A A   G

B A G   B A G   G G A A   B G   B A   G

the right hand

When teaching the Tonette to children, it is possible that following the learning and playing of the tones G, A, and B, they will experiment on their own and play the next two higher tones, namely C, and D. The reason it is not advocated at this point is that at this early stage of playing, the instrument should be held firmly, and by playing C and D all fingers must be removed from the instrument, making position control very difficult.

the tone F

Again play the tone G. (Cover tone holes 1, 2, and 3.) Now add the index finger of the right hand. This is tone F. The tone F is produced by covering tone holes 1, 2, 3, and 4.

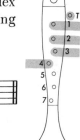

the tone E

Finger the tone F and add the middle finger of the right hand. This produces the tone E. E is produced by covering tone holes 1, 2, 3, 4, and 5.

45

exercises using E, F, and G

the tone D

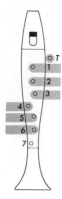

Finger the tone E and add the ring finger of the right hand. This produces the tone D. D is produced by covering tone holes 1, 2, 3, 4, 5, and 6.

THE TONE (low) D

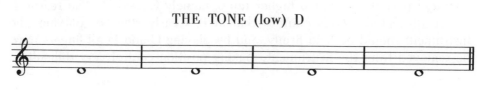

the tone C

The lowest tone one can produce on the instrument is low C. This is played by covering *all* the tone holes (1, 2, 3, 4, 5, 6, and 7). Low C is probably the most difficult tone to produce and the reason it is sometimes hard to play is that all the tone holes are not properly covered. KEEP THE TONE HOLES TIGHTLY COVERED! Also, blow easily into the instrument. These low notes are produced best when played softly.

If the tone is not clear, work down to it like this.

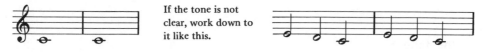

low note exercises

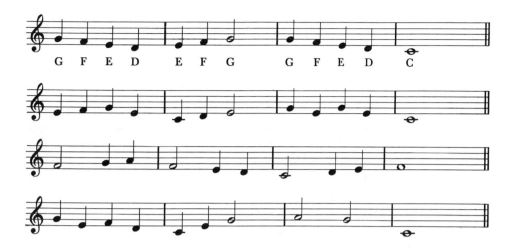

other tones to be learned

After all the tones produced by covering the right-hand tone holes have been learned, it is assumed that the students will have sufficient control of the instrument to play the high C and D with ease, hence it is at this point that those tones should be taught.

the tone C

The tone C is produced by covering only the thumb hole (T).

THE TONE (high) C

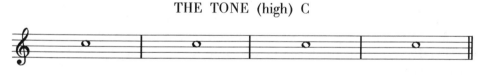

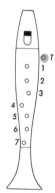

the tone D

The highest tone playable on the Tonette is D. This tone is produced by removing all fingers. To keep the instrument from falling with all fingers removed from the tone holes, the instrument can be held by pressing the upper parts of the index fingers against the instrument.

THE TONE (high) D

It is possible to play all the chromatic tones between the lowest *C* and the *D* a ninth above, but many are not entirely satisfactory. A fingering chart is given (p. 112) which shows you how to finger all of these tones, but it is suggested that one emphasize only two such altered tones, namely the F sharp and the B flat.

the tone F sharp

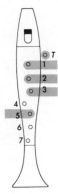

To produce the tone F sharp, one should first finger G (tone holes 1, 2, and 3). Now, instead of lowering G a full step by adding the index finger of the right hand, use instead the middle finger. This will lower the tone from G only a half step, thus producing a raised F, or, correctly stated, an F sharp. F sharp is produced by covering tone holes T, 1, 2, 3, and 5 (not 4).

the tone B flat

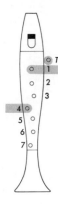

The other chromatic pitch to be considered is B flat. In teaching all chromatic tones, it is best to start from the tone above and work down, rather than to approach the tone from below. If, therefore, one wishes to learn about a lowered B, that is, B flat, start with the natural B (fingered T and 1 tone holes). Now lower that tone a half step. To play an A is to lower it a full step, thus we must produce a pitch halfway between B and A. This is done by fingering B and then adding the index finger of the *right hand* to the natural B fingering. This will produce the desired half step below B.

Therefore, B flat is produced by covering tone holes T, 1, and 4. (Do not cover 2 and 3.)

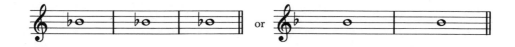

songs to play on the Tonette

On the following several pages are short, easy songs which can be played on the various kinds of whistle flutes. There are many songs which can be played on these instruments, limited only by the restrictions listed below. Look over the songs in any of the basic series of songbooks and discover how many can be played by these simple instruments. The number is great.

Songs can be played on the Tonette if they meet the following criteria:

1. The range of the song is not below middle C nor above fourth-line D.
2. If a song is written in the keys of C, G, or F, and contains no other accidentals, there is no problem. Songs containing more than one sharp or one flat can be played, but the results are not always satisfactory, and generally it is best to avoid such songs.

Two final suggesions:

1. It is not possible to build a precision instrument for the very small price of the average plastic whistle flute. Therefore, both the quality of tone and the accuracy of the pitch produced may sometimes be below hoped-for standards. The best that can be done is to try to develop as clear and accurate a tone as possible.
2. Encourage the children to experiment with the instrument. There is nothing wrong in "playing by ear"; in fact, to do so is frequently a sign of real musical talent. What must be avoided is that the children rely *solely* on their ear and do not learn to read the musical notation.

short practice songs

I KNOW WHERE I'M GOIN'

TOM DOOLEY

ODE TO JOY

GOOD KING WENCESLAS

CUCKOO

CRUEL WAR

songs to
play and sing

index of songs

ABDULLAH BULBUL AMIR

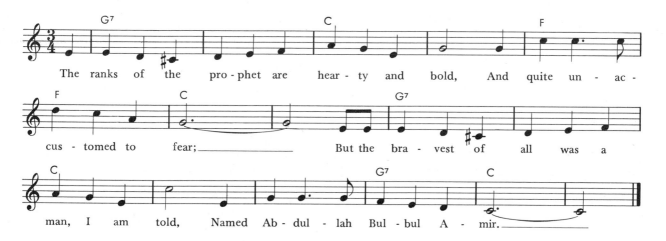

The ranks of the pro-phet are hear-ty and bold, And quite un-ac-cus-tomed to fear;_____ But the bra-vest of all was a man, I am told, Named Ab-dul-lah Bul-bul A-mir._____

2. When they needed a man to encourage the van,
   Or to harass a foe from the rear,
   Storm fort or redoubt, they had only to shout
   For Abdullah Bulbul Amir.

3. This son of the desert in battle aroused,
   Could split twenty men on his spear.
   A terrible creature when sober or soused,
   Was Abdullah Bulbul Amir.

4. Now the heroes were plenty and men known to fame,
   Who fought in the ranks of the Czar;
   But the bravest of these was a man by the name
   Of Ivan Skavinsky Skivar.

5. He could sing like Caruso, play poker and pool,
   And strum on the Spanish guitar;
   In fact, quite the cream of the Muscovite team
   Was Ivan Skavinsky Skivar.

6. The ladies all loved him, his rivals were few;
   He could drink them all under the bar.
   As gallant or tank, there was no one to rank
   With Ivan Skavinsky Skivar.

7. One day this bold Russian had shouldered his gun,
   And walked on the streets with a sneer;
   Downtown he did go, where he trod on the toe
   Of Abdullah Bulbul Amir.

8. "Young man," quoth Bulbul, "has your life grown so dull
   That you're anxious to end your career?
   Vile infidel, know, you have trod on the toe
   Of Abdullah Bulbul Amir."

9. "So take your last look at the sunshine and brook,
   And send your regrets to the Czar,
   By which I imply, you are going to die,
   Mr. Ivan Skavinsky Skivar."

10. Said Ivan, "My friend, your remarks in the end
    Will avail you but little, I fear;
    For you ne'er will survive to repeat them alive,
    Mr. Abdullah Bulbul Amir."

11. Then that bold Mameluke drew his trusty skibouk,
    With a great cry of "Allah Akbar."
    And with murderous intent, he ferociously went
    For Ivan Skavinsky Skivar.

12. They parried and thrust, they sidestepped and cussed,
    Of blood they spilled a great part;
    The philologist blokes, who seldom crack jokes,
    Say that hash was first made on that spot.

13. They fought all that night, 'neath the pale yellow moon,
    The din, it was heard from afar,
    And huge multitudes came, so great was the fame
    Of Abdul and Ivan Skivar.

14. As Abdul's long knife was extracting the life,
    In fact he had shouted, "Huzzah,"
    He felt himself struck by that wily Calmuck
    Count Ivan Skavinsky Skivar.

15. The whistling skibouk did like lightning descend
    And caught Ivan right over the ear,
    While the sabre of Ivan pressed right through the heart
    Of Abdullah Bulbul Amir.

16. The sultan drove by in his red-breasted fly,
    Expecting the victor to cheer,
    But he only drew nigh just to hear the last sigh
    Of Abdullah Bulbul Amir.

17. Czar Petrovich, too, in his spectacles blue,
    Rode up in his new-crested car;
    He arrived just in time to exchange a last line
    With Ivan Skavinsky Skivar.

18. There's a tomb rises up where the Blue Danube rolls,
    And 'graved there in characters clear
    Are, "Stranger, when passing, oh pray for the soul
    Of Abdullah Bulbul Amir."

19. A splash in the Black Sea one dark moonless night
    Caused ripples to spread wide and far.
    It was made by a sack fitting close to the back
    Of Ivan Skavinsky Skivar.

20. A Muscovite maiden, her lone vigil keeps
    'Neath the light of the pale polar star,
    And the name that she shrieks so oft' as she weeps,
    Is Ivan Skavinsky Skivar.

ALL NIGHT, ALL DAY

All night, all____ day, An-gels watch-ing o-ver me, my Lord,____
All night, all____ day, An-gels watch-ing o-ver me. *Fine*

Verse
Now I lay me down__ to sleep, An-gels watch-ing o-ver me, my Lord.__
Pray the Lord my soul__ to keep, An-gels watch-ing o-ver me. *D.C.*

2. *If I die before I wake, Angels watching over me, my Lord.*
Pray the Lord my soul to take, Angels watching over me. (Chorus)

ALOUETTE

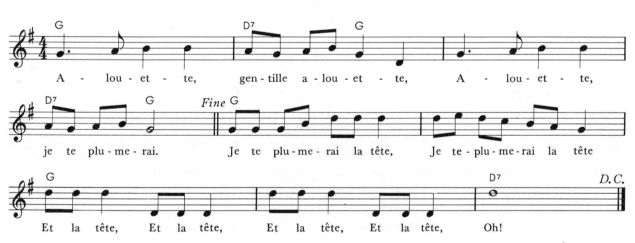

A - lou-et - te, gen - tille a - lou - et - te, A - lou-et - te,
je te plu-me-rai. *Fine* Je te plu-me-rai la tête, Je te-plu-me-rai la tête
Et la tête, Et la tête, Et la tête, Et la tête, Oh! *D.C.*

AULD LANG SYNE

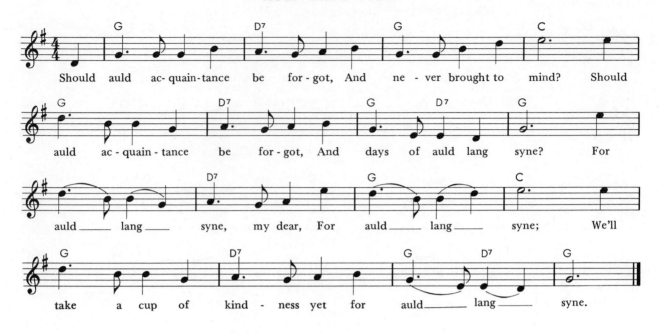

Should auld ac-quain-tance be for-got, And ne-ver brought to mind? Should

auld ac-quain-tance be for-got, And days of auld lang syne? For

auld____ lang____ syne, my dear, For auld____ lang____ syne; We'll

take a cup of kind-ness yet for auld____ lang____ syne.

BILE THEM CABBAGE DOWN

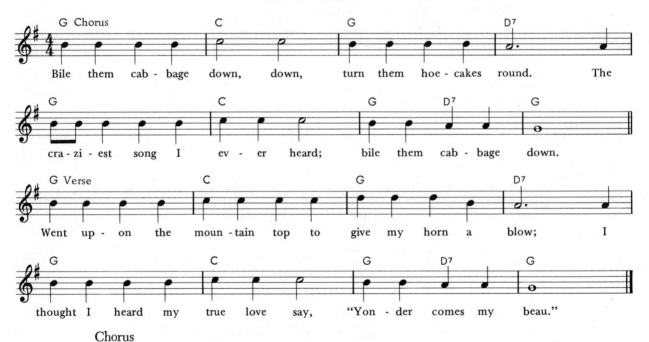

Bile them cab-bage down, down, turn them hoe-cakes round. The

cra-zi-est song I ev-er heard; bile them cab-bage down.

Went up-on the moun-tain top to give my horn a blow; I

thought I heard my true love say, "Yon-der comes my beau."

Chorus
> *Bile them cabbage down, down; turn them hoecakes 'round.*
> *The craziest song I ever heard; bile them cabbage down.*

Verse
2. *Took my gal to the blacksmith shop to have her mouth made small;*
   She turned around a time or two and swallowed shop and all.

3. *Possum in a 'simmon tree, raccoon on the ground,*
   Raccoon says, "You son-of-a-gun, shake some 'simmons down."

4. *Someone stole my ol' 'coon dog, wish they'd bring him back,*
   He chased the big hogs through the fence, the little ones through the crack.

5. *Met a possum in the road, blind as he could be,*
   Jumped the fence and whipped my dog and bristled up at me.

6. *Once I had an ol' gray mule, his name was Simon Slick,*
   He'd roll his eyes and back his ears, and how that mule would kick.

7. *How that mule would kick. He kicked with his dyin' breath;*
   He shoved his hind feet down his throat and kicked himself to death.

8. *I've heard some folks tell there's gold in them thar hills,*
   But I live there for forty years and all I seen was stills.

9. *There's gold up in them hills, I know it for the truth,*
   For my gal she fell down up there and lost her new front tooth.

BILLY BOY

Oh,___ where have you been, Bil - ly Boy, Bil - ly Boy; Oh,___ where have you been, charm - ing Bil - ly?___ I have been to see my wife, she's the joy___ of my life; She's a young thing and can - not leave her moth - er___

2. *Where does she live?*
   She lives on the hill, forty miles from the mill.

3. *Did she bid you to come in?*
   Yes, she bade me to come in, and to kiss her on the chin.

4. *Did she take your hat?*
   Yes, she took my hat, and she threw it at the cat.

5. *Did she set for you a chair?*
   Yes, she set for me a chair, but the bottom wasn't there.

6. *Can she bake a cherry pie?*
   She can bake a cherry pie, quick as a cat can wink her eye.

7. *Can she make a feather bed?*
   She can make a feather bed, that will rise above your head.

8. *How old is she?*
   She's three times six, four times seven, twenty-eight and eleven.

BINGO

There was a far - mer had a dog, And Bin - go was his name - O

B - I - N - G - O, B - I - N - G - O,

B - I - N - G - O, And Bin - go was his name - O.

BLOW THE WIND

Blow the wind south - er - ly, south - er - ly, south - er - ly,

Blow the wind south o'er the bon - ny blue sea; Blow the wind south - er - ly,

south - er - ly, south - er - ly, Blow, bon - ny breez - es, my dear ones to me.

They told me last night there were ships in the off - ing, And

I hur - ried down to the deep roll - ing sea; But my eyes could not see it, where -

ev - er might be it, The bark that is bear - ing my dear ones to me.

THE BLUE–TAIL FLY

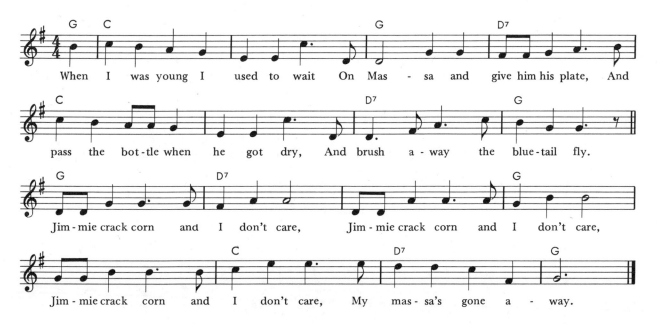

When I was young I used to wait On Mas - sa and give him his plate, And
pass the bot-tle when he got dry, And brush a - way the blue-tail fly.
Jim - mie crack corn and I don't care, Jim - mie crack corn and I don't care,
Jim - mie crack corn and I don't care, My mas - sa's gone a - way.

2. *And when he'd ride in the afternoon, I'd follow with a hickory broom;*
The pony being rather shy When bitten by the blue-tail fly. (Chorus)

3. *One day he rode around the farm, The flies so numerous they did swarm;*
One chanced to bite him on the thigh; The devil take the blue-tail fly. (Chorus)

4. *The pony he run, he jump, he pitch, He threw my massa in the ditch.*
He died, and the jury wondered why; The verdict was the blue-tail fly. (Chorus)

5. *They lay him under a 'simmon tree; His epitaph is there to see:*
"Beneath this stone I'm forced to lie, A victim of the blue-tail fly." (Chorus)

BOLD SOLDIER

2. "Soldier, oh soldier, it's I should be your bride,
   But for fear of my father some danger might betide."
   Then he pulled out sword and pistol, and he hung them by his side,
   And swore they would be married no matter what betide. (Chorus)

3. Then he took her to the parson, and of course then home again,
   There they met her father and seven arm-ed men.
   "Let us fly," said the lady, "for I fear we shall be slain."
   "Hold your hand," said the soldier, "and never fear again." (Chorus)

4. Then he pulled out sword and pistol and caused them to rattle;
   The lady held the horses while the soldier fought in battle.
   "Hold your hand," said the old man, "and do not be so bold,
   And you shall have my daughter and a thousand pounds of gold." (Chorus)

5. "Fight on," said the lady, "For the portion is too small."
   "Hold your hand," said the old man, "and you shall have it all."
   Then he took them right straight home, and he called them son and dear,
   Not because he loved them, but only through fear. (Chorus)

BUFFALO GALS

As I was walk - ing down the street, Down the street, down the street, A

pret - ty li'l gal I chanced to meet, Un - der the sil - v'ry moon.

Chorus

Buf - fa - lo gals won't you come out to - night, Come out to - night, come out to - night

Buf - fa - lo gals won't you come out to - night, And dance by the light of the moon.

2. *I asked her if she'd stop and talk, Stop and talk, stop and talk.*
   Her feet took up the whole sidewalk, She was fair to view. (Chorus)

3. *I asked her if she'd be my wife, Be my wife, be my wife.*
   Then I'd be happy all my life, If she'd marry me. (Chorus)

BOW BELINDA

Bow, bow, bow Be - lin - da; Bow, bow, bow Be - lin - da;

Bow, bow, bow Be - lin - da; Won't you be my dar - ling?

CAN'T YOU DANCE THE POLKA?

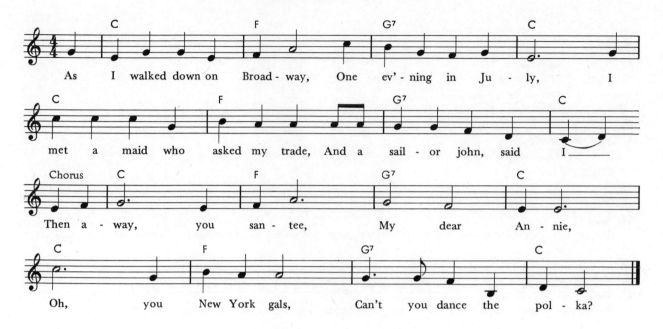

As I walked down on Broad - way, One ev' - ning in Ju - ly, I

met a maid who asked my trade, And a sail - or john, said I____

Chorus Then a - way, you san - tee, My dear An - nie,

Oh, you New York gals, Can't you dance the pol - ka?

2. *To Tiffany's I took her, I did not mind expense,*
   I bought her two gold earrings, They cost me fifty cents. (Chorus)

3. *Says she, "You limejuice sailor, Now see me home you may."*
   But when we reached her cottage door She unto me did say: (Chorus)

4. *"My young man he's a sailor, With his hair cut short behind;*
   He wears a tarry jumper, And he sails the Black Ball Line." (Chorus)

CINDY

Oh, have you seen my Cin - dy? She comes from 'way down south, And
she's so sweet the hon - ey - bees, Just swarm a - round her mouth. Get a - long
home, Cin - dy, Cin - dy, Get a - long home, Cin - dy, Cin - dy; Get a - long
home, Cin - dy, Cin - dy, I'll mar - ry you some - day.

2. *The first time I saw Cindy She was standing in the door,*
   Her shoes and stockings in her hands, Her feet all over the floor. (Chorus)

3. *She told me that she loved me, She called me sugarplum,*
   She threw her arms around my neck, I thought my time had come. (Chorus)

4. *I wish I had a needle, As fine as I could sew,*
   I'd sew that gal to my coat-tail, And off to town I'd go. (Chorus)

5. *I went to see my Cindy, Carried a pair of shoes,*
   Asked her if she'd marry me, She said she couldn't refuse. (Chorus)

6. *She took me to the parlor, She cooled me with a fan,*
   She said I was the prettiest thing, In the shape of mortal man. (Chorus)

7. *Preacher in the pulpit, Preaching mighty bold,*
   Preaching for the money, To save the sinner's soul. (Chorus)

8. *I wish I was an apple, A-hanging on a tree,*
   And every time my Cindy passed, She'd take a bite of me. (Chorus)

9. *I'll never marry Cindy, Tell you the reason why,*
   Her neck's so long and stringy, I'm afraid she'll never die. (Chorus)

10. *Cindy in the springtime, Cindy in the fall,*
    If I can't have my Cindy, I'll have no girl at all. (Chorus)

11. *Cindy got religion, She had it once before,*
    But when she heard my old guitar, She was the first one on the floor. (Chorus)

CLEMENTINE

Oh, my dar - ling, oh my dar - ling, oh my dar - ling Clem - en - tine, You are
lost and gone for - ev - er, dread - ful sor - ry, Clem - en - tine.

1. *In a cavern, in a canyon, excavating for a mine,*
   Dwelt a miner, forty-niner, and his daughter Clementine.

2. *Oh my darling, oh my darling, oh my darling Clementine,*
   You are lost and gone forever, dreadful sorry, Clementine.

3. *Light she was, and like a fairy, and her shoes were number nine,*
   Herring boxes without topses, sandals were for Clementine.

4. *Drove she ducklings to the water every morning just at nine,*
   Hit her foot against a splinter, fell into the foaming brine.

5. *Ruby lips above the water, blowing bubbles soft and fine,*
   Alas for me I was no swimmer, so I lost my Clementine.

6. *In a churchyard near the canyon, where the myrtle doth entwine,*
   There grow roses and other posies, fertilized by Clementine.

7. *Then the miner, forty-niner, soon began to peak and pine;*
   Thought he oughta "jine" his daughter, now he's with his Clementine.

8. *In my dreams she still doth haunt me, robed in garments soaked with brine;*
   Though in life I used to hug her, now she's dead I draw the line.

9. *How I missed her, how I missed her, how I missed my Clementine,*
   'Til I kissed her little sister, and forgot my Clementine.

COCKLES AND MUSSELS

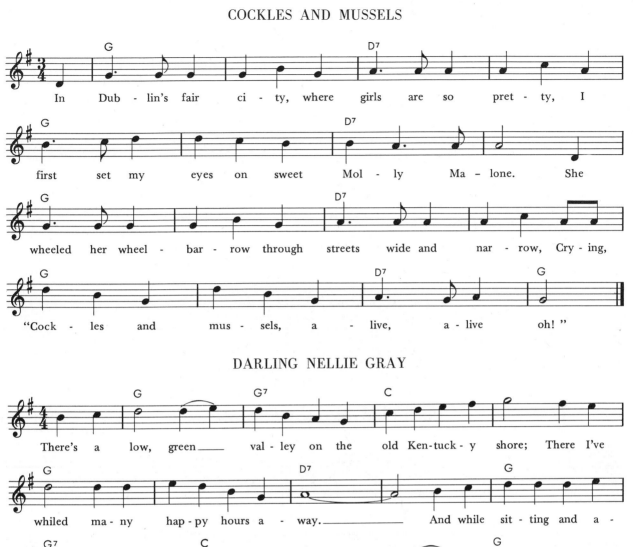

In Dub-lin's fair ci-ty, where girls are so pret-ty, I first set my eyes on sweet Mol-ly Ma-lone. She wheeled her wheel-bar-row through streets wide and nar-row, Cry-ing, "Cock-les and mus-sels, a-live, a-live oh!"

DARLING NELLIE GRAY

There's a low, green valley on the old Ken-tuck-y shore; There I've whiled ma-ny hap-py hours a-way. And while sit-ting and a-sing-ing by the lit-tle cot-tage door, Where lived my dar-ling Nel-lie Gray. Oh my dar-ling Nel-lie Gray they have ta-ken her a-way. And I'll ne-ver see my darl-ing an-y more. I'm a sit-ting by the ri-ver and I'm weep-ing all the day For you've gone from the old Ken-tuck-y shore.

DARLING, YOU CAN'T LOVE ONE

Darl - ing, you can't love one,_____ Darl - ing, you can't love one,_____ You can't love one and have an - y fun, Oh, Darl - ing, you can't love one._____

2. *Darling, you can't love two, (2 times)*
You can't love two and still be true,
Oh, Darling, you can't love two.

3. *Darling, you can't love three, (2 times)*
You can't love three and stay here with me,
Oh, Darling, you can't love three.

THE DEAF WOMAN'S COURTSHIP

Old wo - man, old wo - man, Will you do my wash - ing?
Old wo - man, old wo - man, Will you do my wash - ing?
Speak a lit - tle loud - er, sir, I'm ve - ry hard of hear - ing.
Speak a lit - tle loud - er, sir, I'm ve - ry hard of hear - ing.

2. *Old woman, old woman, Will you do my ironing?*
Old woman, old woman, Will you do my ironing?
Speak a little louder, sir, I'm very hard of hearing.
Speak a little louder, sir, I'm very hard of hearing.

3. *Old woman, old woman, Will you do my mending?*
Old woman, old woman, Will you do my mending?
Speak a little louder, sir, I'm very hard of hearing.
Speak a little louder, sir, I'm very hard of hearing.

4. *Old woman, old woman, Do you want to marry me?*
   Old woman, old woman, Do you want to marry me?
   Oh, my goodness gracious, sir, I hear you very clearly.
   Oh, my goodness gracious, sir, I hear you very clearly.

DONA NOBIS PACEM

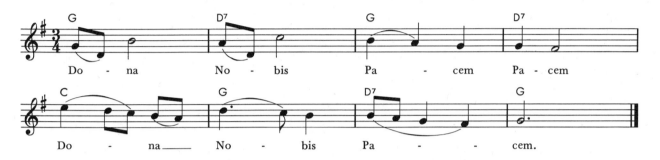

DOWN IN THE VALLEY

2. *Roses love sunshine, violets love dew,*
   Angels in heaven know I love you.
   Know I love you, dear, know I love you,
   Angels in heaven know I love you.

3. *If you don't love me, love whom you please,*
   Throw your arms 'round me, give my heart ease.
   Give my heart ease, love, give my heart ease,
   Throw your arms 'round me, give my heart ease.

4. *Write me a letter, send it by mail,*
   Send it in care of the Birmingham Jail.
   Birmingham Jail, Birmingham Jail,
   Send it in care of the Birmingham Jail.

5. *Build me a castle forty feet high,*
   So I can see her as she rides by.
   As she rides by, love, as she rides by,
   So I can see her as she rides by.

6. *Writing this letter, containing three lines,*
   Answer my question, "Will you be mine?"
   Will you be mine, love, will you be mine?
   Answer my question, "Will you be mine?"

DRILL, YE TARRIERS, DRILL

Ev - 'ry morn-ing at sev - en o' - clock there were twen - ty tar - ri - ers a - work-ing at the rock, And the boss comes a - long and he says, "Keep still, and come down hea - vy on the cast iron drill." And drill, ye tar - ri - ers, drill. And drill, ye tar - ri - ers, drill, Oh, it's work all day for the su - gar in your "Tay," Down be - hind the rail - way, And drill, ye tar - ri - ers, drill, and blast, and fire.

2. *Our new foreman was Dan McCann,*
   I'll tell you true, he was a real mean man;
   Last week a premature blast went off,
   And a mile in the air went Big Jim Goff. (Chorus)

3. *Next time payday came around*
   Jim Goff was short one buck, he found,
   When he asked, "What for?" came this reply,
   "You're docked for the time you were up in the sky." (Chorus)

4. *The boss was a fine man down to the ground,*
   And he married a lady six feet round;
   She baked good bread and she baked it well,
   But she baked it hard as the holes in hell. (Chorus)

ELIZA JANE

There's a girl in Bal - ti - more, E - li - za Jane, She's the one that I a - dore, E - li - za Jane. Oh, E - li - za, E - li - za Jane, Oh, E - li - za, E - li - za Jane.

E–RI–E CANAL

We were for-ty miles from Al-ba-ny, for-get it I nev-er shall; What a ter-ri-ble storm we had one night on the E-ri-e Ca-nal. The E-ri-e was a-ris-ing, the gin was a-get-tin' low, And I scarce-ly think we'll get a drink 'til we get to Buf-fa-lo, _____ 'Til we get to Buf-fa-lo.

2. We were loaded down with barley, We were chock up full of rye,
   And the captain he looked down on me With his doggone wicked eye. (Chorus)

3. The captain he came up on deck, With a spy glass in his hand,
   And the fog it was so gosh darned thick That he couldn't spy the land.

4. Three days out from Albany A pirate we did spy,
   The black flag with the skull and bones was wavin' up on high.

5. We signaled to the driver To hoist the flag of truce,
   And we found it was the Mary Jane Just out of Syracuse.

6. Two days out from Syracuse The vessel struck a shoal,
   And we like to all been drowned On a chunk o' Lackawanna coal.

7. We hollered to the captain On the towpath, treadin' dirt;
   He pumped on board and stopped the leak With his old red flannel shirt.

8. Our cook she was a grand old gal, She had a ragged dress;
   We hoisted her upon a pole As a signal of distress.

9. When we got to Syracuse, The off-mule he was dead;
   The nigh mule got blind staggers, And we cracked him on the head.

10. The captain he got married, And the cook she went to jail,
    And I'm the only son-of-a-gun That's left to tell the tail.

FIVE HUNDRED MILES

If you miss the train I'm on, you will know that I am gone. You can hear the whis - tle blow five hun - dred miles, ___ ___ Five hun - dred miles, five hun - dred miles, five hun - dred miles, five hun - dred miles. You can hear the whis - tle blow five hun - dred miles. ___

2. *Lord, I'm one, Lord, I'm two, Lord, I'm three, Lord, I'm four,*
   Lord, I'm five hundred miles from my home.
   Away from home, away from home, away from home, away from home,
   Lord, I'm five hundred miles away from home.

3. *Not a shirt on my back, not a penny to my name,*
   No, I can't go home this away,
   This away, this away, this away, this away,
   No, I can't go home this away.

FOGGY, FOGGY DEW

When I was a bach'-lor, I lived all a-lone, I worked at the wea-ver's trade;___ And the on-ly, on-ly thing that I did that was wrong, Was to woo a fair young maid. I wooed her in the win-ter-time,___ Part of the sum-mer, too; And the on-ly, on-ly thing that I did that was wrong, Was to keep her from the fog-gy, fog-gy dew.

2. One night she knelt close by my side
   When I was fast asleep.
   She threw her arms around my neck,
   And then began to weep.
   She wept, she cried, she tore her hair,
   Ah, me! what could I do?
   So all night long I held her in my arms,
   Just to keep her from the foggy, foggy dew.

3. Again I am a bach'lor, I live with my son,
   We work at the weaver's trade;
   And every single time that I look into his eyes,
   He reminds me of the fair young maid.
   He reminds me of the wintertime,
   Part of the summer, too,
   And of the many, many times that I held her in my arms,
   Just to keep her from the foggy, foggy dew.

THE FOX

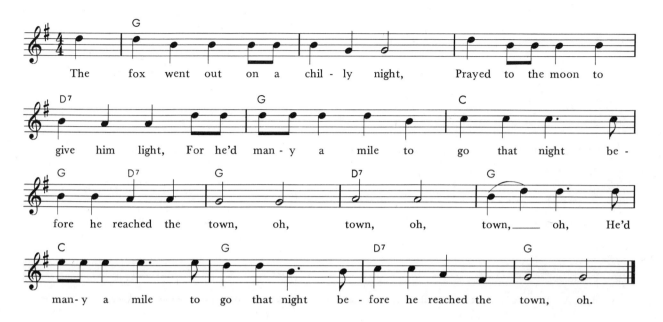

The fox went out on a chil-ly night, Prayed to the moon to give him light, For he'd man-y a mile to go that night be-fore he reached the town, oh, town, oh, town,____ oh, He'd man-y a mile to go that night be-fore he reached the town, oh.

2. *He ran 'til he came to a great big pen,*
   Where the ducks and the geese were kept therein,
   A couple of you will grease my chin
   Before I leave this town, oh. . .

3. *He grabbed the gray goose by the neck,*
   Throwed a duck across his back;
   He didn't mind the quack, quack, quack,
   And the legs all dangling down, oh. . .

4. *The old Mrs. Flipper-Flopper jumped out of bed,*
   Out of the window she cocked her head,
   Saying, "John, John, the goose is gone,
   And the fox is on the town, oh. . ."

5. *The fox he ran to the top of the hill,*
   Blowed his horn both loud and shrill;
   Fox, he said, "I better flee with my kill,
   Or they'll soon be on my trail, oh. . ."

6. *He ran 'til he came to his cozy den,*
   There were the little ones eight, nine, ten;
   They said, "Daddy, better go back again,
   'Cause it must be a mighty fine town, oh. . ."

7. *The fox and his wife without any strife,*
   Cut up the goose with a carving knife;
   They never had such a supper in their life,
   And the little ones chewed on the bones, oh. . .

GOOD NIGHT, LADIES

Good night, la - dies, good night, la - dies,
good night, la - dies, We're going to leave you now.
Mer - ri - ly we roll a - long, roll a - long, roll a - long,
Mer - ri - ly we roll a - long, o'er the deep blue sea.

GREEN CORN

Green corn, come a - long Char - lie, Green corn, don't cha tell Pol - ly,
Green corn, come a - long Char - lie Green corn, don't cha tell Pol - ly.
All I want in this cre - a - tion, Pret - ty lit - tle wife and a big plan - ta - tion.

Chorus

Green corn, come along Charlie,
Green corn, don'tcha tell Polly,
Green corn, come along Charlie,
Green corn, don'tcha tell Polly.

2. *All I need in this creation,*
   Three months work and nine vacation.

3. *Tell my boss any old time,*
   Daytime's his but nighttime's mine.

GREEN GROW THE LILACS

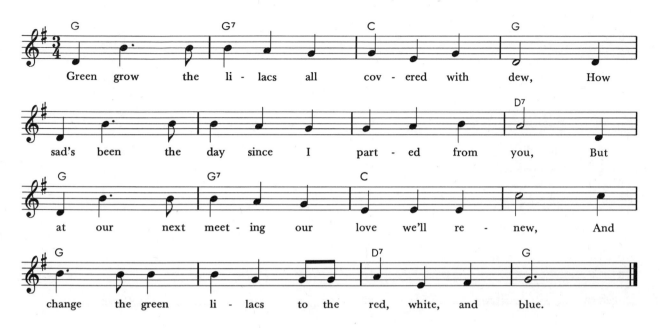

Green grow the li-lacs all cov-ered with dew, How
sad's been the day since I part-ed from you, But
at our next meet-ing our love we'll re-new, And
change the green li-lacs to the red, white, and blue.

2. I once had a sweetheart but now I have none,
She's gone far and left me to live all alone,
Since she's gone and left me, contented I'll be,
For she loves another one better than me.

3. On top of the mountain where green lilacs grow,
And deep in the valley where still waters flow,
I met my true love and she proved to be true,
We changed the green lilacs to the red, white, and blue.

GREENSLEEVES

A - las my love_____ you do me wrong_____ to cast me out so dis - cour - teous - ly. For I have loved_____ you so long_____ de - light - ing in_____ your comp - a - ny. Green - sleeves_____ is all my joy_____ Green - sleeves_____ is my de - light. Green - sleeves is my heart of gold_____ and who but my la - dy Green - sleeves.

GYPSY DAVEY

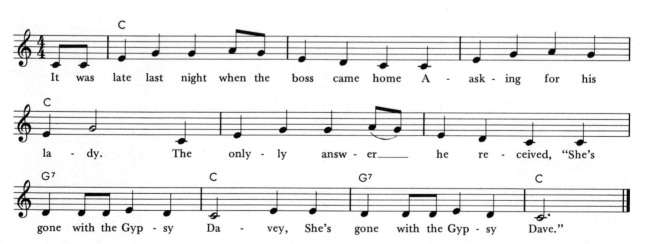

It was late last night when the boss came home A - ask - ing for his la - dy. The on - ly - ly answ - er_____ he re - ceived, "She's gone with the Gyp - sy Da - vey, She's gone with the Gyp - sy Dave."

2. *"Go saddle me my buckskin horse*
And hundred-dollar saddle.
Point out to me their wagon tracks
And after them I'll travel,
And after them I'll ride."

3. *I had not rode to the midnight moon*
   When I saw campfire gleaming.
   I heard the notes of the big guitar
   And the voice of the gypsies singing
   That song of the Gypsy Dave.

4. *There in the light of the camping fire,*
   I saw her fair face beaming.
   Her heart in tune to the big guitar
   And the voice of the gypsies singing
   That song of the Gypsy Dave.

5. *"Have you forsaken your house and home,*
   Have you forsaken your baby?
   Have you forsaken your husband dear
   To go with the Gypsy Davey,
   To sing with the Gypsy Dave?"

6. *"Yes, I've forsaken my husband dear*
   To go with the Gypsy Davey,
   And I've forsaken my mansion high
   But not my blue-eyed baby,
   But not my blue-eyed babe."

7. *She smiled to leave her husband dear*
   And go with the Gypsy Davey;
   But the tears come a-tricklin' down her cheeks
   To think of the blue-eyed baby,
   Pretty little blue-eyed babe.

8. *"Take off, take off your buckskin gloves*
   That are made of Spanish leather;
   And give to me your lily white hand
   And we'll ride home together,
   And we'll ride home again."

9. *"No, I won't take off my buckskin gloves,*
   That are made of Spanish leather.
   I'll go my way from day to day
   And sing with the Gypsy Davey,
   That song of the Gypsy Dave."

HAPPY BIRTHDAY

Patti Hill
Mildred Hill

Hap - py birth - day to you. Hap - py birth - day to you. Hap - py

birth - day dear - - - Hap - py birth - day to you.

HE'S GOT THE WHOLE WORLD IN HIS HANDS

He's got the whole world ____ in his hands, ____ He's got the whole world ____ in his hands, ____ He's got the whole world ____ in his hands, ____ He's got the whole world in his hands.

2. *He's got the wind and rain in His hands.*

3. *He's got that little bitty baby in His hands.*

4. *He's got you and me in His hands.*

5. *He's got everybody in His hands.*

THE HUNCHBACK FIDDLER

There once was a fidd-ler in Frank-furt a' Main. His back had a hump but his fidd-ling was fine. On the way to his house he crossed ____ a ____ square, he crossed a ____ square. A crowd of love-ly la - dies was ga - ther - ing there.

2. *You poor hunchback fiddler come play us a tune.*
We promise to grant you a worthiest boon.
Play a polka or waltz so gay and bright, so gay and bright,
For we are celebrating Walpurgis tonight.

3. *The fiddler began; how the fiddle did sing.*
The ladies went dancing around in a ring.
When the fiddler had played the final chord, the final chord,
One lady said, "Oh, Fiddler, come claim your reward."

4. *She tapped on his shoulder and counted to ten.*
The fiddler stood slender and tall once again.
"Oh, I'll fiddle no more," cried he with glee, cried he with glee,
"For now the lovely ladies will go dancing with me."

HUSH, LITTLE BABY

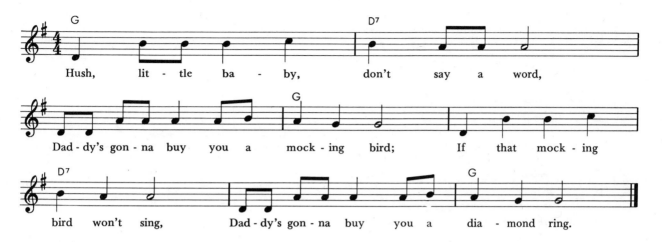

Hush, lit-tle ba-by, don't say a word,
Dad-dy's gon-na buy you a mock-ing bird; If that mock-ing
bird won't sing, Dad-dy's gon-na buy you a dia-mond ring.

2. *If that diamond ring turns brass,*
   Daddy's gonna buy you a looking glass;
   If that looking glass gets broke,
   Daddy's gonna buy you a billy goat.

3. *If that billy goat won't pull,*
   Daddy's gonna buy you a cart and bull;
   If that cart and bull turn over,
   Daddy's gonna buy you a dog named Rover.

4. *If that dog named Rover won't bark,*
   Daddy's gonna buy you a horse and cart;
   If that horse and cart fall down,
   You'll be the sweetest little girl in town.

IF YOU'RE HAPPY

If you're hap-py and you know it wear a smile, If you're
hap-py and you know it wear a smile. If you're hap-py and you know it Then your
life will sure-ly show it, If you're hap-py and you know it wear a smile.

2. If you're happy and you know it clap your hands,
   If you're happy and you know it clap your hands.
   If you're happy and you know it
   Then your life will surely show it,
   If you're happy and you know it clap your hands.

3. If you're happy and you know it tap your feet,
   If you're happy and you know it tap your feet.
   If you're happy and you know it
   Then your life will surely show it,
   If you're happy and you know it tap your feet.

I WAS BORN ABOUT TEN THOUSAND YEARS AGO

I was born a-bout ten thou-sand years a-go, There ain't
noth-ing in this world that I don't know, I saw Pe-ter, Paul, and Mo-ses play-ing
ring a-round the ro-ses, And I'll whip the guy that says it is-n't so.

2. I saw Satan when he looked the garden o'er,
   I saw Eve and Adam driven from the door,
   And behind the bushes peeping, saw the apple they were eating,
   And I swear that I'm the guy that ate the core.

3. I taught Samson how to use his mighty hands,
   Showed Columbus this happy land,
   And for Pharaoh's little kids I built the pyramids,
   And to Sahara I carried all the sand.

4. I taught Solomon his little ABC's,
   I was the first guy to eat limburger cheese,
   And while sailing down the bay with Methuselah one day,
   I saw his whiskers a-floating in the breeze.

5. I saw Jonah when he shoved off in the whale,
   And I thought he'd never live to tell the tale,
   But old Jonah'd eaten garlic, so he gave the whale the colic,
   And he coughed him up and let him out of jail.

6. I saw Absalom a-hanging by the hair,
   When they built the wall of China I was there,
   I saved King Solomon's life and he offered me a wife,
   I said, "Now you're talking business, have a chair."

7. I saw Israel in the battle of the Nile,
   The arrows were flying thick and fast and wild,
   I saw David with his sling pop Goliath on the wing,
   I was doing forty seconds to the mile.

8. I saw Samson when he laid the village cold,
   I saw Daniel tame the lions in their hold,
   I helped build the Tower of Babel up as high as they were able,
   And there's lots of other things I haven't told.

9. Queen Elizabeth she fell in love with me,
   We were married in Milwaukee secretly,
   But I snuck around and shook her, to go off with General Hooker,
   To fight skeeters way down in Tennessee.

I WISH I WAS SINGLE AGAIN

I wish I was sin - gle a - gain,_____ I wish I was

sin - gle a - gain,_____ Oh, when I was sin - gle, my

pock - ets would jin - gle; I wish I was sin - gle a - gain._____

2. I married a wife, oh then,
   I married a wife, oh then,
   I married a wife, she's the curse of my life;
   I wish I was single again.

3. My wife, she died, oh then, (repeat)
   My wife, she died, and I laughed 'til I cried,
   To think I was single again.

4. I went to the funeral, and danced Yankee Doodle,
   To think I was single again.

5. I married another, the devil's grandmother,
   I wish I was single again.

6. She beat me, she banged me, she said she would hang me,
   And I wish I was single again.

7. She went for the rope, when she got it, 'twas broke,
   And I wish I was single again.

8. Now lend me your ears, young men, (repeat)
   Be good to the first, for the second's much worse,
   And I wish I was single again.

82

I'VE BEEN WORKING ON THE RAILROAD

JENNIE JENKINS

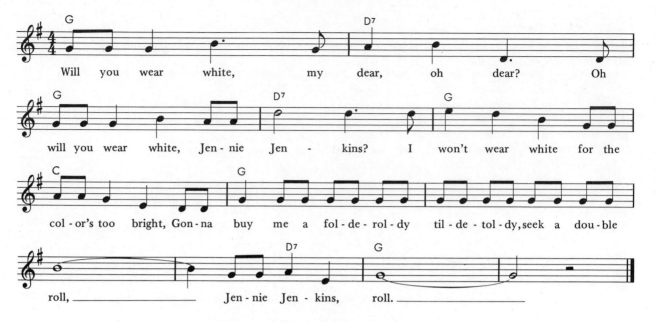

Will you wear white, my dear, oh dear? Oh will you wear white, Jen-nie Jen-kins? I won't wear white for the col-or's too bright, Gon-na buy me a fol-de-rol-dy til-de-tol-dy, seek a dou-ble roll, _____ Jen-nie Jen-kins, roll. _____

2. *Will you wear red, my dear, oh dear?*
   Oh will you wear red, Jennie Jenkins?
   I won't wear red, it's the color of my head; etc.

3. *Will you wear blue, my dear, oh dear?*
   Oh will you wear blue, Jennie Jenkins?
   I won't wear blue, cause the color's too true; etc.

4. *Will you wear green, my dear, oh dear?*
   Oh will you wear green, Jennie Jenkins?
   I won't wear green, it's a shame to be seen; etc.

5. *Will you wear purple, my dear, oh dear?*
   Oh will you wear purple, Jennie Jenkins?
   I won't wear purple, it's the color of my turtle; etc.

6. *Will you wear black, my dear, oh dear?*
   Oh will you wear black, Jennie Jenkins?
   I won't wear black, it's the color of my back; etc.

7. *What will you wear, my dear, oh dear?*
   Oh what will you wear, Jennie Jenkins?
   I have nothing to wear, I can't go anywhere; etc.

JESSE JAMES

Jes-se James was a lad who killed many a man; He robbed the Glen-dale

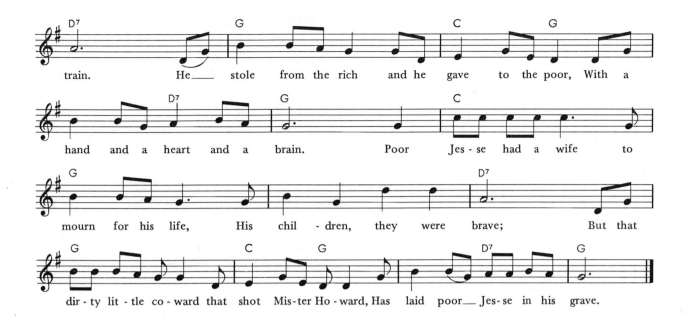

train. He stole from the rich and he gave to the poor, With a
hand and a heart and a brain. Poor Jes-se had a wife to
mourn for his life, His chil-dren, they were brave; But that
dir-ty lit-tle co-ward that shot Mis-ter Ho-ward, Has laid poor Jes-se in his grave.

2. *Poor Jesse had a wife to mourn for his life,*
   His children, they were brave;
   But that dirty little coward that shot Mister Howard,
   Has laid poor Jesse in his grave.

3. *Jesse was a man, a friend to the poor,*
   He never would see a man suffer pain;
   And with his brother Frank he robbed the Chicago bank,
   And stopped the Glendale train.

4. *It was his brother Frank that robbed the Gallatin bank,*
   And carried the money from the town;
   It was in this very place that they had a little race,
   For they shot Captain Sheets to the ground.

5. *They went to a crossing not very far from there,*
   And there they did the same;
   With the agent on his knees, he delivered up the keys,
   To the outlaws, Frank and Jesse James.

6. *It was on a Wednesday night, the moon was shining bright,*
   They stopped the Glendale train;
   And the people they did say, for many miles away,
   It was robbed by Frank and Jesse James.

7. *It was on a Saturday night, Jesse was at home,*
   Talking with his family brave;
   Robert Ford's pistol ball brought him tumblin' from the wall
   And laid poor Jesse in his grave.

8. *The people held their breath when they heard of Jesse's death,*
   And wondered how he came to die,
   It was one of the gang called little Robert Ford,
   He shot poor Jesse on the sly.

JOHN JACOB JINGLEHEIMER SCHMIDT

John Ja - cob Jin - gle - hei - mer Schmidt, His name is my name too, When - ev - er we go out, The peo - ple al - ways shout, "John Ja - cob Jin - gle - hei - mer Schmidt." Da da da da da da da

KUM BA YA

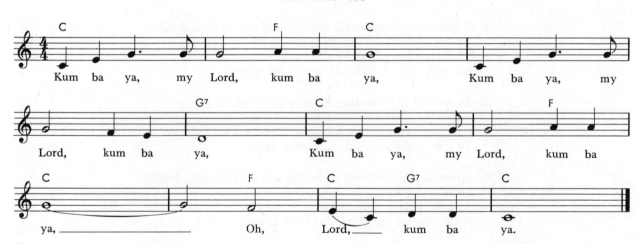

Kum ba ya, my Lord, kum ba ya, Kum ba ya, my Lord, kum ba ya, Kum ba ya, my Lord, kum ba ya, Oh, Lord, kum ba ya.

2. *Someone's sleeping, Lord, kum ba ya, etc.*

3. *Someone's crying, Lord, kum ba ya, etc.*

4. *Someone's praying, Lord, kum ba ya, etc.*

5. *Someone's singing, Lord, kum ba ya, etc.*

MICHAEL FINIGIN

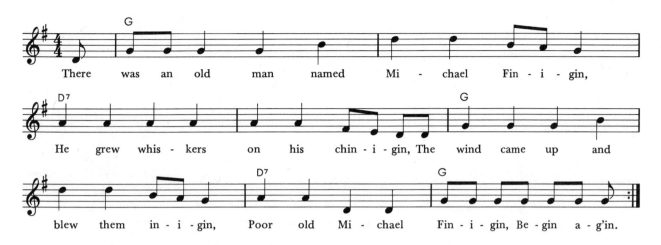

There was an old man named Mi - chael Fin - i - gin,
He grew whis - kers on his chin - i - gin, The wind came up and
blew them in - i - gin, Poor old Mi - chael Fin - i - gin, Be - gin a - g'in.

2. *There was an old man named Michael Finigin,*
   He went fishing with a pinigin,
   He caught a fish but dropped it inigin,
   Poor old Michael Finigin. Begin agin'.

3. *There was an old man named Michael Finigin,*
   Climbed a tree and ruined his shinigin,
   He took off many years of skinigin,
   Poor old Michael Finigin. Begin agin'.

4. *There was an old man named Michael Finigin,*
   He grew fat and then grew thinigin,
   He died and then had to beginigin,
   Poor old Michael Finigin. The endigin.

MICHAEL, ROW THE BOAT ASHORE

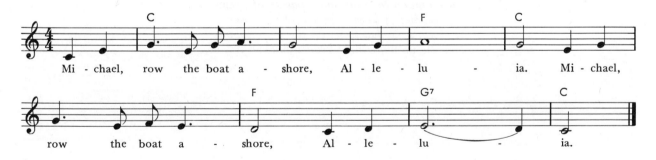

Mi - chael, row the boat a - shore, Al - le - lu - ia. Mi - chael,
row the boat a - shore, Al - le - lu - ia.

2. *Sister, help to trim the sail, Alleluia.*

3. *Jordan river's deep and wide, Alleluia.*

4. *Jordan river's chilly and cold, Alleluia.*

OH, DEAR, WHAT CAN THE MATTER BE?

Oh, Dear, what can the matter be? Oh, Dear, what can the matter be? Oh, Dear, what can the matter be? Johnny's so long at the fair. He pro - mised to buy me a trin - ket to please me, And then for a kiss, oh he vowed he would tease me, He pro - mised to bring me a bunch of blue rib - bons To tie up my bon - nie brown hair, So it's

Oh, Dear, what can the matter be?
Oh, Dear, what can the matter be?
Oh, Dear, what can the matter be?
Johnny's so long at the fair.

2. *He promised to bring me a basket of posies,*
   An arm full of lilies, a bunch of red roses,
   A pretty straw hat to set off the blue ribbons
   That tie up my bonnie brown hair. So it's, etc.

OH, MARY, DON'T YOU WEEP

Oh, Ma-ry, don't you weep, don't you mourn; Oh, Ma-ry, don't you weep, don't you mourn;

Pha-raoh's ar-my got drown-ded, Oh, Ma-ry, don't you weep.

If I could I sure-ly would stand on the rock where Mo-ses stood.

Pha-raoh's ar-my got drown-ded, Oh, Ma-ry, don't you weep.

2. If I could I surely would Stand on the rock where Moses stood.
   Pharaoh's army got drownded, Oh, Mary, don't you weep.

3. Wonder what Satan's a-grumblin' 'bout, Chained in Hell an' he can't get out.

4. Ol' Satan's mad and I am glad, Missed that soul he thought he had.

5. I went down in the valley to pray, My soul got happy and I stayed all day.

6. Brother, better mind how you walk on the Cross, Foot might slip and your soul get los'.

7. God told Noah to build him an ark, Noah built the ark outa hick'ry bark.

8. One of these nights about twelve o'clock, This old world's gonna reel and rock.

9. Now don't you believe the Bible ain't true, 'Cause you'll be sorry if you do.

10. That primrose path is wide and fair, Many a soul's done perished there.

ON TOP OF OLD SMOKEY

On top of Old Smo - key, _____ All cov - ered with snow, _____ I

lost my true lo - ver _____ From court - ing too slow. _____

2. Oh courting is pleasure And parting is grief,
   And a false-hearted lover Is worse than a thief.

3. A thief will just rob you And take what you have,
   But a false-hearted lover Will lead to the grave.

4. Your grave will decay you And turn you to dust,
   Not one boy in fifty That a poor girl can trust.

5. They'll hug you and kiss you, And tell you more lies,
   Than the raindrops from heaven Or stars in the skies.

6. They'll swear that they love you Your heart just to please,
   As soon as your back's turned, They'll love whom they please.

7. Just as sure as the dew falls All on the green corn,
   Last night he was with me, This morning he's gone.

LITTLE MOHEE (same tune as "On Top of Old Smokey")

1. As I was out walking Upon a fine day,
   I got awful lonesome, As the day passed away.

2. I sat down amusing Alone on the grass,
   When who should sit by me But a young Indian lass.

3. She sat down beside me, Took hold of my hand,
   Said, "You are a stranger And in a strange land."

4. "But if you will follow, You're welcome to come,
   And dwell in the cottage That I call my home."

5. The sun was fast sinking Far over the sea,
   As I wandered along With the lassie Mohee.

6. She asked me to marry, And gave me her hand
   Saying, "Father's a chieftain All over this land."

7. "Oh no, my dear maiden That never can be,
   'Cause I have a sweetheart In my own country."

8. "I will not forsake her, I know she loves me,
   Her heart is as true As any Mohee."

9. *The last time I saw her, She knelt on the sand,*
And as my boat passed her She waved me her hand.

10. *But when I had landed No one could I see*
That did really compare With the little Mohee.

11. *The girl I had trusted Proved untrue to me,*
So I sailed o'er the ocean To my little Mohee.

12. *I turned back my courses And backward I roved,*
To dwell with my Mohee In the coconut grove.

PAPER OF PINS

I'll give to you a pa - per of pins, And that's the way our
love be - gins, If you will mar - ry me, me, me, If you will mar - ry me.

2. *I'll not accept your paper of pins*
If that's the way your love begins,
And I'll not marry you, you, you,
And I'll not marry you.

3. *I'll give to you a dress of red,*
Stitched all 'round with golden thread,
If you will marry me, me, me,
If you will marry me.

4. *I'll not accept your dress of red,*
Stitched all 'round with golden thread,
And I'll not marry you, you, you,
And I'll not marry you.

5. *I'll give to you my house and land,*
Twenty-five cattle and my hired man,
If you will marry me, me, me,
If you will marry me.

6. *I'll not accept your house and land,*
Your cattle, though the offer's grand,
I'd love to have your hired man
But I won't marry you.

7. *I'll give to you the key to my chest,*
And all the money that I possess,
If you will marry me, me, me,
If you will marry me.

8. *I'll take your cash, your key, and chest,*
For God's sake now please let me rest.
Oh, yes, I'll marry you, you, you,
But only for a week or two.

PUTTING ON THE STYLE

2. Sweet sixteen and goes to church just to see the boys;
   Always laughs and giggles at every little noise.
   She turns this way a little, then turns that way awhile,
   But we know she's only putting on the style. (Chorus)

3. Young man in a restaurant smokes a dirty pipe;
   Looking like a pumpkin that's only half-way ripe.
   Smoking, drinking, chewing, thinking all the while
   That there is nothing equal to putting on the style.

4. *Preacher in the pulpit shouting with all his might,*
   Glory Hallelujah—put the people in a fright.
   You might think that Satan's coming up the aisle,
   But it's only the preacher putting on the style.

5. *Young man just from college makes a big display*
   With a great big word which he can hardly say;
   It can't be found in Webster's and won't be for awhile,
   But we know he's only putting on the style.

RED RIVER VALLEY

Come and sit by my side if you love me, Do not has-ten to bid me a-dieu, But re-mem-ber the Red Ri-ver Val-ley, And the cow-boy that loved you so true.

2. *From this valley they say you are going,*
   We will miss your bright eyes and sweet smile,
   For they say you are taking the sunshine
   That has brightened our pathway awhile.

3. *Won't you think of the valley you're leaving?*
   Oh, how lonely, how sad it will be,
   Oh, think of the fond heart you're breaking,
   And the grief you are causing to me.

4. *From this valley they say you are going;*
   When you go, may your darling go, too?
   Would you leave me behind unprotected,
   When I love no other but you?

5. *As you go to your home by the ocean,*
   May you never forget those sweet hours,
   That we spent in the Red River Valley,
   And the love we exchanged 'mid the flowers.

RIDDLE SONG

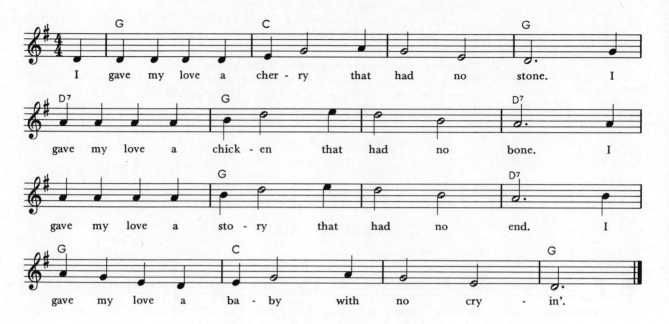

I gave my love a cher-ry that had no stone. I
gave my love a chick-en that had no bone. I
gave my love a sto-ry that had no end. I
gave my love a ba-by with no cry-in'.

2. How can there be a cherry that has no stone?
How can there be a chicken that has no bone?
How can there be a story that has no end?
How can there be a baby with no cryin'?

3. A cherry when it's blooming it has no stone.
A chicken when it's pippin' it has no bone.
The story that I love you it has no end.
A baby when it's sleeping has no cryin'.

SANDY LAND

Make my liv-ing in San - dy Land, Make my liv-ing in San - dy Land,
Make my liv-ing in San - dy Land, La - dies, fare you well.

2. Digging potatoes in Sandy Land, etc.

3. One more river I'm bound to cross, etc.

4. How are you my pretty little miss? etc.

SHE'LL BE COMING 'ROUND THE MOUNTAIN WHEN SHE COMES

2. *She'll be driving six white horses when she comes, etc.*

3. *Oh, we'll all go out to meet her when she comes, etc.*

4. *Oh, we'll kill the old red rooster when she comes, etc.*

5. *Oh, we'll all have chicken and dumplings when she comes, etc.*

SKIP TO MY LOU

Flies in the but-ter-milk, shoo fly shoo.
Flies in the but-ter-milk, shoo fly shoo. Flies in the but-ter-milk,
shoo fly shoo. Skip to my Lou, my darl - ing.

2. *If you can't get a redbird, a bluebird'll do.*

3. *I've lost my girl, now what'll I do?*

4. *I'll get another, a better one too.*

5. *When I go courting, I take two.*

6. *My girl wears a number nine shoe.*

7. *I'll get another one sweeter than you.*

8. *Kitten in the haymow, mew, mew, mew.*

9. *I'll get her back in spite of you.*

10. *We'll keep it up 'til half past two.*

11. *Stole my partner, skip to my Lou.*

SO LONG, IT'S BEEN GOOD TO KNOW YOU

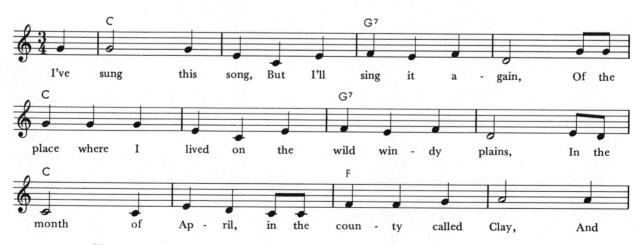

I've sung this song, But I'll sing it a - gain, Of the
place where I lived on the wild win - dy plains, In the
month of Ap - ril, in the coun - ty called Clay, And

96

here's what all of the peo - ple there say. Well it's

so long, it's been good to know you, So

long, it's been good to know you, So long, it's

been good to know you, This dus - ty old dust is a - get -ting my

home, And I've got to be drift - ing a - long._____

2. *That dust storm hit, and it hit like thunder,*
   It dusted us over and covered us under,
   It blocked off the traffic and covered the sun,
   And straight for home all the people did run, singing, (Chorus)

3. *Two sweethearts sat in the dark and they sparked,*
   They hugged and they kissed in the dusty old dark,
   They sighed and cried and hugged and kissed,
   Instead of marriage they talked like this, they said, (Chorus)

4. *The telephone rang and it jumped off the wall,*
   That was the preacher, a-making his call,
   He said, "Kind friends, this must be the end,
   You've got your last chance at salvation from sin, then it's, (Chorus)

5. *The church was jammed, the church was packed,*
   That dusty old dust storm, it blowed so black,
   The preacher could not read a word of his text,
   So he folded his specs and he took up collection, singing, (Chorus)

SOW TOOK THE MEASLES

When I was young I bought me a plough, A couple of chick-ens and a lit-tle black sow. Chick-ens or ducks or an-y such thing, The sow took the mea-sles and she died in the spring.

2. *What do you think I made of her hide?*
   The very best saddle that you ever did ride.
   Saddle or bridle or any such thing,
   The sow took the measles and she died in the spring.

3. *What do you think I made of her nose?*
   The very best thimble that ever sewed clothes.
   Thimble or thread or any such thing,
   The sow took the measles and she died in the spring.

4. *What do you think I made of her feet?*
   The very best pickles that you ever did eat.
   Pickles or glue or any such thing,
   The sow took the measles and she died in the spring.

SPRINGFIELD MOUNTAIN

On Spring-field Moun-tain there did dwell, A love-ly youth, I knew him well. Oh tu-le-lu-ri-lu-ri lay, Oh tu-le-lu-ri-lu-ri lay.

2. *This lovely youth one day did go*
   Down to the meadow for to mow. (Chorus)

3. *Just once around, and he did feel*
   A pizen sarpent strike his heel. (Chorus)

4. *He laid right down upon the ground,*
   Shut both his eyes and looked around. (Chorus)

5. *They took him home to Molly dear,*
   For he did feel so very queer. (Chorus)

6. *Now Molly had two ruby lips*
   With which the pizen she did sip. (Chorus)

7. *But Molly had a rotten tooth,*
   And so the pizen killed them both. (Chorus)

8. *Come all young men and warning take,*
   Don't ever get bit by a rattlesnake. (Chorus)

STREETS OF LAREDO

As I _____ walked out in the streets of La - re - do, As
I walked out in La - re - do one day, I
spied a young cow - boy all wrapped in white li - nen, All
wrapped in white li - nen as cold as the clay.

2. *"I see by your outfit that you are a cowboy."*
   These words he did say as I boldly walked by,
   "Come sit down beside me and hear my sad story;
   I'm shot in the chest and I know I must die.

3. *"It was once in the saddle I used to go dashing,*
   Once in the saddle I used to go gay;
   First down to Rosie's and then to the card-house;
   I'm shot in the chest and I'm dying today.

4. *"Get sixteen gamblers to carry my coffin;*
   Six pretty maidens to sing me a song;
   Take me to the green valley and lay the sod o'er me;
   I'm just a young cowboy and I know I've done wrong.

5. *"Oh, beat the drum slowly and play the fife lowly,*
   Play the dead march as they carry me along;
   Put bunches of roses all over my coffin,
   Roses to deaden the clods as they fall."

SWEET BETSY FROM PIKE

Oh do you re-mem-ber sweet Bet-sy from Pike? She

crossed the big moun-tain with her lo-ver Ike, With

two yoke of ox-en, a big yal-ler dog, A

tall Shang-hai roos-ter and one spot-ted hog.

Chorus

Hoo-dle-dang fol-de-di-do, hoo-dle-dang, fol-de-day.

2. *They swam the wild rivers and climbed the tall peaks,*
   And camped on the prairies for weeks upon weeks,
   Starvation and cholera, hard work and slaughter,
   They reached California, spite of hell and high water. (Chorus)

3. *They soon reached the desert where Betsy gave out,*
   And down in the sand she lay rolling about,
   While Ike he gazed at her with sobs and with sighs,
   Saying, "Get up now, Betsy, you'll get sand in your eyes." (Chorus)

4. *The Indians came down in a wild yelling horde,*
   And Betsy got skeered they would scalp her adored,
   So behind the front wagon wheel Betsy did crawl,
   And fought off the Indians with musket and ball. (Chorus)

5. *They stopped off at Salt Lake to inquire the way,*
   And Brigham declared that sweet Betsy should stay,
   But Betsy got frightened and ran like a deer,
   While Brigham stood pawing the ground like a steer. (Chorus)

6. *One morning they climbed up a very high hill,*
   And with wonder looked down upon old Placerville,
   Ike shouted and said as he cast his eyes down,
   "Sweet Betsy, my darling, we've got to Hangtown." (Chorus)

7. *The Shanghai ran off, and the cattle all died,*
   The last piece of bacon that morning was fried,
   Ike got discouraged and Betsy got mad,
   The dog wagged his tail and looked wonderfully sad. (Chorus)

8. *Long Ike and Sweet Betsy attended a dance,*
Where Ike wore a pair of his best Sunday pants,
And Betsy was covered with ribbon and rings,
Said Ike, "You're an angel, but where are your wings?" (Chorus)

9. *A miner said, "Betsy, will you dance with me?"*
"I will, you ole hoss, if you won't make too free,
But don't dance me hard, do you want to know why?
Doggone you, I'm chock full of strong alkali." (Chorus)

10. *Long Ike and Sweet Betsy got married, of course,*
But Ike, getting jealous, obtained a divorce,
While Betsy, well satisfied, said with a shout,
"Goodbye, you big lummox, I'm glad you backed out." (Chorus)

THERE IS A TAVERN IN THE TOWN

There is a tav-ern in the town, in the town, And there my true love sits him down, sits him down— And— drinks his wine as mer-ry as can be, And nev-er, nev-er thinks of me. Fare thee well, for I must leave thee do not let our part-ing grieve thee, And re-mem-ber that the best of friends must part, must part, A-dieu, a-dieu, Kind friends a-dieu, yes, a-dieu, I can no long-er stay with you, stay with you—I'll— hang my heart on a weep-ing wil-low tree, And may the world go well with thee.—

2. *He left me for a damsel sweet, damsel sweet,*
Each Friday night they used to meet, used to meet,
And now my love who once was true to me,
Takes this sweet damsel on his knee. (Chorus)

3. *And now I see him nevermore, nevermore,*
He never knocks upon my door, on my door,
Oh, woe is me, he penned a little note,
And these were all the words he wrote: (Chorus)

4. *Oh, dig my grave both wide and deep, wide and deep,*
Put tombstones at my head and feet, head and feet,
And on my breast you may carve a turtle dove,
To signify I died for love. (Chorus)

101

THERE WAS AN OLD WOMAN

There was an old wo-man who swal-lowed a fly, And
I don't know why she swal-lowed a fly, Per-haps she'll die.
There was an old wo-man who swal-lowed a spi-der that
wigg-led and jigg-led and tick-led in-side her,
She swal-lowed the spi-der to swal-low a fly, And I don't know
why she swal-lowed the fly, Per-haps she'll die.

Ending
There was an old wo-man who swal-lowed a horse; She's dead of course.

2. *There was an old woman who swallowed a spider*
   That wiggled and jiggled and tickled inside her,
   She swallowed the spider to swallow a fly,
   And I don't know why she swallowed the fly,
   Perhaps she'll die.

3. *There was an old woman who swallowed a bird,*
   How absurd to swallow a bird,
   She swallowed a bird to swallow a spider to swallow a fly,
   And I don't know why she swallowed the fly,
   Perhaps she'll die.

4. *There was an old woman who swallowed a cat;*
   Imagine that—to swallow a cat.
   She swallowed a cat to swallow a bird to swallow a spider to swallow a fly,
   And I don't know why she swallowed a fly,
   Perhaps she'll die.

102

5. *There was an old woman who swallowed a dog;*
   What a hog to swallow a dog.
   She swallowed a dog to swallow a cat to swallow a bird to swallow a spider
       to swallow a fly,
   And I don't know why she swallowed a fly,
   Perhaps she'll die.

6. *There was an old woman who swallowed a goat;*
   Just opened her throat and swallowed a goat.
   She swallowed a goat to swallow a dog to swallow a cat to swallow a bird
       to swallow a spider to swallow a fly,
   And I don't know why she swallowed a fly,
   Perhaps she'll die.

7. *There was an old woman who swallowed a cow;*
   I don't know how she swallowed a cow.
   She swallowed a cow to swallow a goat to swallow a dog to swallow a cat
       to swallow a bird to swallow a spider to swallow a fly,
   And I don't know why she swallowed a fly,
   Perhaps she'll die.

Ending:
   There was an old woman who swallowed a horse;
   She's dead of course.

appendix

recorder fingering chart
guitar chord fingerings
Tonette fingering chart

Guitar Chords

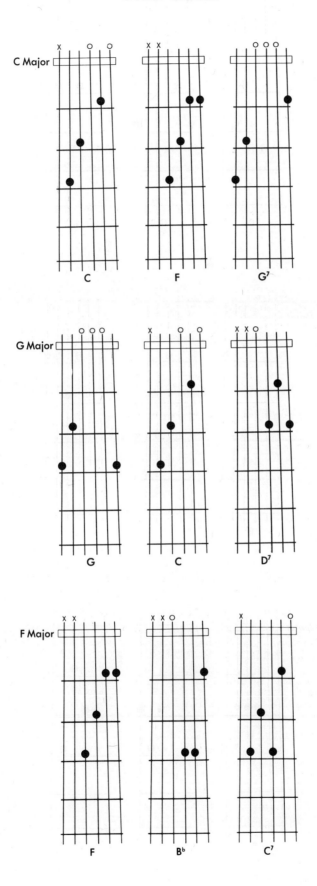

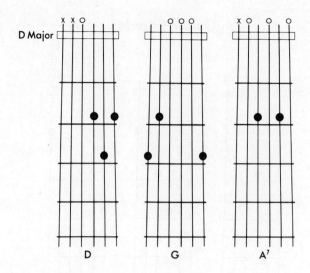

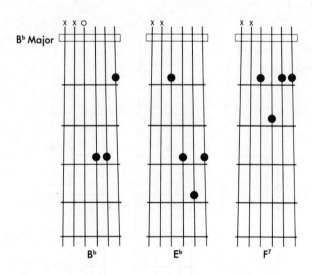

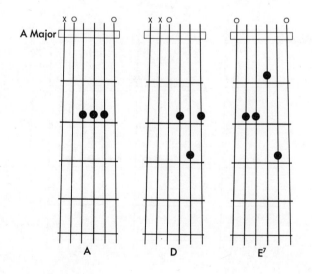

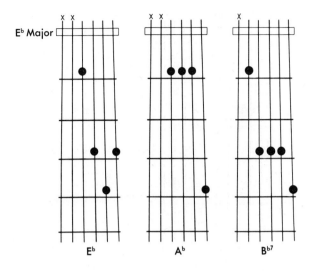

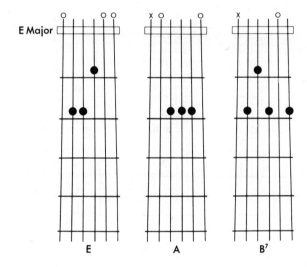

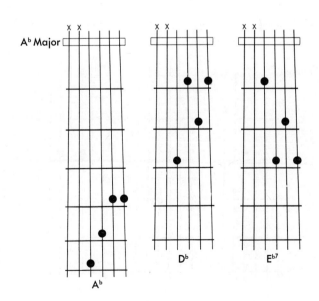

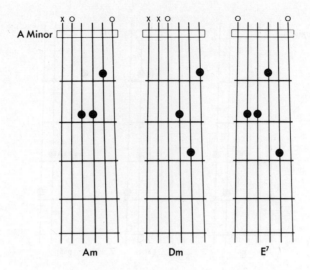

Am   Dm   E⁷

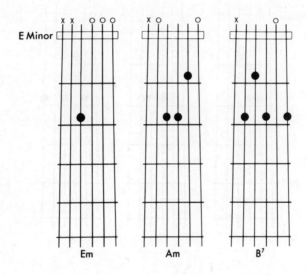

Em   Am   B⁷

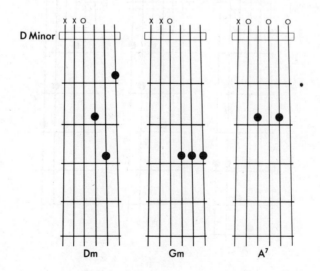

Dm   Gm   A⁷

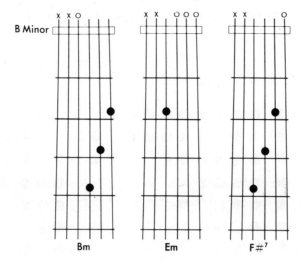

B Minor

Bm   Em   F#⁷

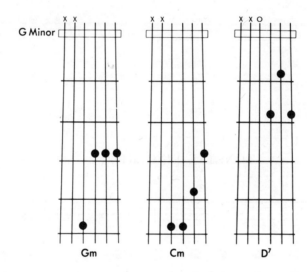

G Minor

Gm   Cm   D⁷

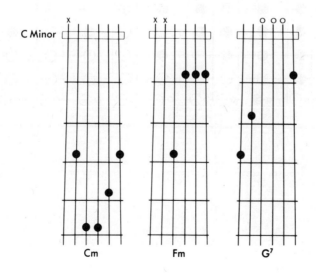

C Minor

Cm   Fm   G⁷

RECORDER FINGERINGS, SOPRANO (C)

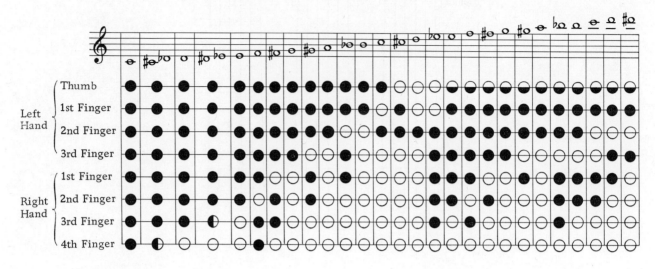

TONETTE FINGERINGS

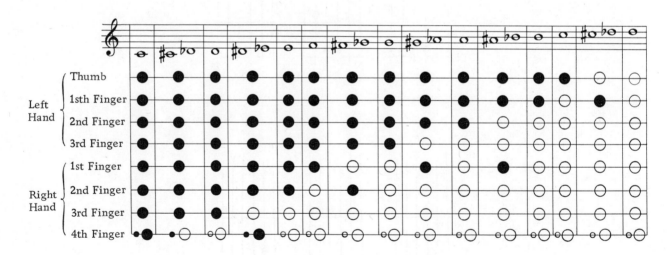